Lifelines 2

COPING SKILLS IN ENGLISH

SECOND EDITION

Barbara Foley

Howard Pomann

Prentice Hall Regents

This series is dedicated to our dear friend and colleague, Gretchen Dowling.

Gretchen Dowling
8/31/43 – 4/13/89

Acquisitions editor: Nancy Leonhardt
Production supervision: Noël Vreeland Carter
Interior design: A Good Thing
    and Jerry Votta
Cover design: Jerry Votta
Illustrations: Don Martinetti, D.M. Graphics, Inc.
Prepress Buyer: Ray Keating
Manufacturing buyer: Lori Bulwin
Scheduler: Leslie Coward

Photo Credits:
Laima Druskis, Units 1, 5, 7, and 17; Teri Leigh Stratford, Units 2 and 6; Hakim Raquib, Units 3, and 20; Florida Department of Commerce, Division of Tourism, Unit 4; Shirley Zeiberg, Unit 8; Don S. Forschmidt, Metropolitan Transportation Authority, Unit 9; Jane Latta, Units 11 and 13; Irene Springer, Unit 15; R. P. Ruddy, Unit 16; American Heart Association, Unit 18; Johnson & Johnson, Unit 19.

Printed in the United States of America
10

ISBN 0-13-529702-8

OVERBROOK PARK

Contents

Introduction

Barbara Foley and Howard Pomann have devised this survival skills series specifically for entry-level adult students who need to learn basic skills and basic language in order to function effectively in the United States. The conversations and practices lead students through carefully controlled exercises to the point where they can "put it together" for themselves. In addition to whole-class and large-group activities, LIFELINES features many small-group activities which allow the teacher to step aside and become a facilitator as the students work together using the language in new and different ways. The focus on coping skills and functional language, rather than grammar and vocabulary, promotes learning by increasing student interest. The repetition of the same basic exercise formats throughout, allows students to concentrate on learning language, not exercise formats. Gretchen Dowling's excellent "To the Teacher" section gives clear explanations of how to do each exercise, along with an abundance of ideas for adapting them to your own individual needs. Photographs, drawings and realia bring the content of each unit to life for students. LIFELINES really makes learning easier for your students, and teaching easier for you.

Sharon Seymour
Alemany Community
College Center
San Francisco

To the Teacher

LIFELINES is a four-book ESL coping skills series for adult learners at entry, beginning, low-intermediate and intermediate levels. Each book deals with ten or more different coping skill areas. The series is competency-based and integrates the coping skills with the essential language forms, vocabulary, and cultural information needed in each situation.

Skill areas are reintroduced throughout the series with different competencies. For example, in "Telephone," in Book 1, students ask to speak with someone; in Book 2, they leave a simple message; in Book 3, they give and take a longer message; in Book 4, they ask for the right person or office. Those competencies requiring simpler language forms come before those calling for more difficult ones. Thus, grammatical points such as verb tenses are introduced in appropriate sequence. They are reintroduced cyclically throughout the series and via the different contexts within each book.

The series is suitable for a wide variety of adult and secondary school classes. It could be the total program, for example, for open-entry ESL classes of 3-6 hours per week. For intensive language courses, it would be one strand of the total program. In community college or secondary school classes, it could be used either to reinforce grammatical structures, or to introduce them in context.

Each unit is self-contained, takes approximately two hours, and affords practice in listening, speaking, reading, and writing. The table of contents for each book lists the coping skill areas, the functions or competencies, and the main grammatical structures in each chapter. This gives the teacher easy access to the information needed to choose how best to integrate LIFELINES with individual programs, classes, and teaching styles.

The series incorporates both whole class and small group learning activities. All the activities are designed to give students as much "inner space" as possible to process the language according to their own individual learning styles. Those for the whole class are to introduce or sum up the structure, vocabulary, and cultural information needed to perform the coping skill; those for the small groups, to provide students with the intensive independent practice they need to make the language their own.

In the whole class activities, the teacher utilizes stories, pictures, and conversations to introduce the new language and information in the chapter. Although the teacher is leading the activity, the activities are designed so that the teacher can easily elicit the correct language with minimal teacher modeling.

In small group activities, the teacher's role is that of a small group facilitator assisting the students in completing their tasks, rather than that of a leader. Depending on the activity and level of the students, a teacher can circulate from group to group, stay with one group, or sit separately from the groups and assist only when asked.

Students working in small groups learn to discover their own mistakes, to correct each other, to share opinions, to experiment with the language, and to work as a learning community. Small groups allow the teacher to divide the class according to particular language needs, and to work with students having individual problems as well as those who are ahead of the class. They also free students to ask questions they may not ask in the whole class setting.

For the teacher, one of the biggest advantages of LIFELINES is that small group work, and accommodation to different learning styles, are built-in. It is not necessary to supplement the books with small group tasks in order to meet individual student needs. The small group activities have been tested with a wide variety of students. They work without extra work for the teacher.

Naturally, there are many ways to handle the activities presented in the workbooks, depending on students' proficiency levels, and the teacher's personal style. In the pages which follow, the authors offer "how to" suggestions which have proven effective for them. These are intended simply as some ways to structure classwork so that students have maximum opportunity to meet their own learning needs in a productive and secure atmosphere. They are not intended as limits on the readers' style or creativity.

WHOLE CLASS ACTIVITIES

Discuss

Discuss

The Discuss questions and accompanying illustration or photo set the scene for the unit. The class should talk about the illustration and what they see happening in the picture. The Discuss questions help the student to relate their personal opinions and experiences to the theme of the unit. Cultural comments and explanations can be made at this time. During this introduction to the unit, the focus is on expanding the students' knowledge of the coping skill rather than the correction of grammar.

Listen, Read and Say

Listen, Read and Say

This is the dialogue which introduces the language and competency. It is the core from which all the other activities and expansions in the chapter emerge. Thus, it is vital that the meaning be clear to the students.

Step 1: Students read the dialogue to themselves and figure out as much of the meaning as they can on their own. During this process, they can talk to each other and even translate. The surer they are that they know what the dialogue says in their own language, the easier it is for them to "let go" and absorb the English. The teacher can circulate, answering individual questions and/or getting a sense of what may be needed to explain to the entire group.

Step 2: When students feel reasonably clear about the meaning, the teacher makes any necessary further clarification, dramatizations, or explanations. The teacher may then want to read the dialogue aloud once or twice while students listen and look at their books. This helps them associate the sound of English with the meanings they have worked out. The dialogue may be written on the board and the students asked to close their books. This serves as a signal to focus on English together.

Step 3: Practice the dialogue. (a) This can be done by the usual choral then individual repetition, followed by half the class taking one speaker's part while half takes the other, culminating with individual students role playing the parts.

(b) A variation or supplement to this is to change the "rules of the game" and have the teacher repeat after the students. The teacher stands at the back of the room, and lets the students, one at a time, call out whatever word, phrase or sentence they want to hear. The teacher repeats the student's utterance until the student stops initiating the repetition. The teacher behaves like a tape recorder with a natural, non-judgmental voice: by just letting the students hear the utterance they "ask" for, the exercise helps them self-correct and develop their own criteria for grammar and pronunciation. If students fail to self-correct an important point, it is best to deal with the point after the exercise, rather than to break the mood of the self-directed learning.

Since this exercise is a bit different from what most classes are accustomed to, it is necessary to explain it clearly beforehand. With very basic classes to whom one cannot translate, it often helps to number the sentences in the dialogue. Then the teacher can say and easily demonstrate, "Tell me the number you want to hear. I will say the sentence. If you say the number again, I will repeat the sentence. I am a machine. I will repeat what you say. I will stop when you say 'stop.' "

(c) As an aid to internalizing the dialogue, the teacher can erase every fifth word and replace it with a line, having students read the dialogue while orally filling in the missing words. This procedure is repeated with lines for every third word, and so on, until students are "reading" a dialogue composed of completely blank lines. Members of the class might then cooperate in filling in all the blanks to reinforce correct spelling, etc.

Practice

This activity introduces new vocabulary within the previously established context and grammatical structures. A single sentence or interaction from the dialogue is given as the model. Students practice the model, substituting the vocabulary cued by the pictures below it.

Step 1: If much of the vocabulary is new, students can repeat each item in isolation, chorally and then individually, following the teacher's model.

Step 2: The teacher elicits the use of the new items within the model sentence or interaction. One way to do this is simply to have the students repeat the complete utterances after the teacher. This is a good first step, especially for very low-level classes. After this initial security is given, however, students need a little more independence.

A variation, or follow-up, is for the teacher to give only the first utterance as a model. The teacher then simply points to or calls out the number of each different picture and has the students give the complete utterance. This can be done both chorally and individually.

Step 3: Students can then continue practicing all the substitutions, with the person sitting next to them. The teacher can circulate, helping with pronunciation as necessary.

Step 4: To further reinforce the pronunciation of the new vocabulary, follow the procedures described in Step 4b of Listen, Read, and Say.

SMALL GROUP ACTIVITIES

Before beginning the small group activities, the teacher divides the students in groups of two to five depending on the activity and the size of the class. The teacher then goes over the directions carefully and demonstrates what each student will do, explaining what the teacher's role will be, whether circulating from group to group, or staying with one group. The teacher should give the students a time frame; for example, telling the students they have fifteen minutes to complete the task. The time frame can always be extended. Clear information about what to expect helps students feel secure and be more productive.

There are many different ways to group students. Some teachers like to have students of the same ability together; others to mix them so the more advanced can help the slower. Some like to mix language backgrounds in order to encourage the use of English; others to have the same backgrounds together in order to raise the security level, or to facilitate students' explaining things to each other. Some like student self-selection so that working friendships may develop more easily; others don't see this as crucial to the development of supportive, productive groups. Each teacher's values and pedagogical purposes will determine the way the class is divided into groups.

Partner Exercise

This small-group activity is designed for two students to practice a specific grammatical structure in a controlled interaction. The left-hand column of the *Partner Exercise* gives word or picture cues from which Student 1 forms a statement or question. The right-hand column gives the complete sentences. Student 2 looks at this column, using it to be "teacher" and check the utterances of the other student. Students are to fold the page in the middle so that S1 is looking at the left-hand column and S2 at the right.

Step 1: The teacher explains all this to the students. One way is to copy two or three items in the left-hand column on one side of the board. (It is not necessary to worry about awkward picture drawing; it usually just provides a few moments of laughter for the class.)

(b) Then draw the corresponding items from the right-hand column on the other side of the board.

(c) The teacher assumes the roles of the two students and demonstrates what each is to do.

(d) The teacher calls for student volunteers to come up to the board, stand in front of the appropriate columns, and do the exercise.

(e) The teacher demonstrates folding the exercise page, and indicates which side each is to look at.

Step 2: Students form into pairs of students.

Step 3: Students fold their pages and do the exercise.

Step 4: The teacher can circulate from group to group assisting when asked or needed, encouraging students to listen carefully and to correct each other's sentences and pronunciation.

Step 5: When a pair has completed the exercise, the two students should change roles and do it again.

Complete

Completion activities provide writing practice and the use of individual cognitive skills. Students are asked, for example, to complete sentences, write questions, fill in forms, find and apply information from charts or maps, etc. Directions are specific for each activity. To explain and structure the activities, the teacher can use the chalkboard. As the students write individually or in small groups, the teacher circulates, giving assistance as needed or requested.

Concentration

The *Concentration* game is designed to practice new vocabulary and to teach discrimination between grammatical structures.

Step 1: The teacher cuts out the picture and word/sentence cards before class. The *Concentration* "deck" can be clipped together by a paper clip or kept in an envelope. The number of "decks" needed will be equal to the number of groups playing.

Step 2: Students sit in groups of three to five. The picture and word/sentence cards are shuffled and placed face down on a desk with the picture cards on one side, and the word/sentence cards on the other. The first player turns up a picture card and says the word or sentence that corresponds to the picture. The player then turns up a word/sentence card trying to match the picture. If the cards match, the student keeps them. If not, they are both replaced face down in the original position. The next student tries to match two cards in the same manner.

Step 3: The play continues until all the cards are matched. The teacher circulates from group to group assisting when asked. When the students finish the game, the teacher checks their cards, pointing out errors, but letting the students make the corrections themselves.

Step 4: An extension of this exercise is to give one student in the group all the word/sentence cards and distribute the picture cards to the other students in the group. The students take turns saying the word or utterance that describes their picture. If they say it correctly, the student with the word/sentence cards gives them the card that matches the picture.

Interaction

Interaction

The Interaction Charts give the students a structured opportunity to practice their new language with one or two other students. Each activity begins with two or more questions about the topic.

Step 1: Students sit with a partner and ask each question. They mark their partner's response on the chart, usually by recording a "yes" or "no," circling an appropriate response or writing a single word. The students then switch roles. Often, other language and questions emerge as the students interact. The teacher should encourage the students to speak freely and gain confidence in their language use.

Step 2: Repeat Step 1 with a different partner. Most interaction charts ask the students to speak with two students.

Step 3: After the students have their partners' responses, several students should report their information back to the class. Typically, the teacher will ask a student, "Who(m) did you speak to?" and "What did he tell you?" The goal in this activity is correctly reporting information and using the new vocabulary. Do not focus on the correctness of the grammar.

Putting It Together

The last page in each unit gives the students the opportunity to practice and expand the coping and language skills emphasized in the unit in a freer mode of conversation. The activities on this page are based on an illustration of the coping skill in a particular situation.

Step 1: A lively illustration depicts the coping skills scene. As a whole class or in small groups, the students write down six to ten vocabulary words from the picture. If the students work in small groups, they then meet together as a whole class and share the lists which each group developed.

Step 2: The students talk about the picture. The teacher should take a low profile role in this activity. If prompting is necessary, he might say, "Talk about _____ (one of the characters in the scene)." A student will usually give just one or two sentences. The teacher should spend a minimum of ten minutes on this activity. Encourage the students to speak, even if the sentences they give are short or the same as those given by other students.

Step 3: Next, the students are asked to answer questions about the picture or to match short conversations about the picture.

When the exercise reads, "Discuss these questions," the students can ask and answer the questions in a small group or as a whole class. This is an oral exercise and the focus is both on correct information and on grammar. As a homework assignment, the students may write the answers to the questions.

When the exercise is matching, the students are asked to match short questions and answers which relate to the picture. As partners, the students memorize both parts of the interaction. Then, in small groups or as a whole class, the students divide into two groups. In Group A, the students look at the entire exercise. In Group B, the students cover the second column. A student from Group A gives the first part of the interaction from the first column. A student from Group B tries to answer or complete the interaction with the response from the second column. Continue until the students are comfortable with all the questions and answers. Then, switch groups.

Step 4: Role plays are the final activity. The students work together as partners and write a conversation about the picture or the coping skill area. The students have the support of the picture, the vocabulary and the questions or matching conversations. The teacher should circulate, giving assistance as needed and requested. The students practice the conversation without looking at their papers, and then stand in front of the class and act out their conversations. Remember that whenever this kind of freedom is given, a teacher may expect less perfection in students' language than he does during controlled practice.

Students may decide to tape record one or more of the conversations with the teacher's assistance. After the students complete the conversation, they can play back the tape one sentence at a time, repeating after the tape and writing the conversation on the chalkboard.

Gretchen Dowling
Barbara H. Foley
Howard Pomann

Acknowledgments

The development of this series has been the result of a long growth process. We wish to thank our many friends and colleagues who have given their support, shared their ideas, and increased our insights into the language-learning process and its application in the ESL classroom:

John Chapman, Ralph Colognori, Joyce Ann Custer, Mary Dolan, John Duffy, Jacqueline Flamm, Irene Frankel, Susan Lanzano, Elaine Langdon, Joann La-Perla, Darlene Larson, Marsha Malberg, Camille Mahon, Fred Malkemes, Joy Noren, Douglas Pillsbury, Deborah Pires, Sherri Preiss, Jennybelle Rardin, Sharon Seymour, Earl Stevick, and the faculty at the Institute for Intensive English, Union College.

And special thanks goes to our spouses, Bill and June, for their patience and love.

Barbara Foley
Howard Pomann

1 The First Day

Discuss

What's the date?
Is this your first day or
    first week of school?
How many students are
    in your class?
What's the name of
    your school?
Is your school large?

Listen, Read and Say

Elena: Hi, Koji. My name's Elena. You sit next to me in class.
  Koji: Yes. Hi. Nice to meet you.
Elena: What country are you from?
  Koji: I'm from Japan.
Elena: How long have you been in the United States?
  Koji: For two years.
Elena: Do you live in San Diego?
  Koji: Yes, I live about two miles from here.
Elena: It's 11:00, time for class. Nice talking with you.

Practice
Practice

Use this model. Introduce yourself to the class.

> I'm _____.
>
> I'm from _____.
>
> I've been in the United States for _____ months/years.
>
> I live in _____.
>
> I'm married/single/divorced.
>
> I have _____ children. *or* I don't have any children.

Ask two students these questions. Fill in their answers on the chart.

QUESTION	STUDENT 1	STUDENT 2
What's your name?		
Where are you from?		
How long have you been in the United States?		
Where do you live?		
Are you married?		
Do you have any children?		

Find out about your school. Ask your teacher about each of these places. Use this model.

Where's the ___*main office*___?

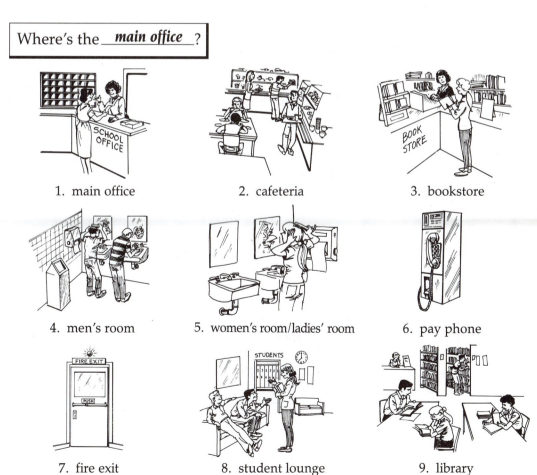

1. main office

2. cafeteria

3. bookstore

4. men's room

5. women's room/ladies' room

6. pay phone

7. fire exit

8. student lounge

9. library

Ask your teacher or another student these questions about school. Write the answers.

1. What's the name of this school? _____
2. Where's the school? _____
3. What's the telephone number of the school? _____
4. What's the room number? _____
5. What's the teacher's name? _____
6. What days do we have class? _____
7. What are the class hours? _____
8. Do we have a break? _____

Practice **Practice**

Practice these common classroom expressions with the teacher. Then decide what each person is saying in the pictures below.

1. Excuse me.
2. Can you repeat that, please?
3. I'm sorry. I can't hear you.
4. I don't understand this word/sentence.
5. Can you explain this to me?
6. What does _____ mean?
7. How do you say _____ in English?
8. How do you spell _____?
9. Can I borrow a _____?
10. Excuse me. Can I go to the bathroom? (High school)
    Excuse me. I'll be right back. (Adult school)

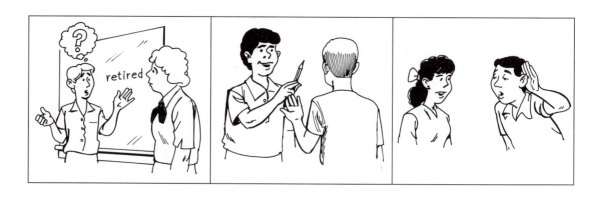

Talk about this classroom. What is each person doing? Write the new vocabulary on the picture.

Discuss these questions.

1. What time is it?
2. Where is the teacher standing?
3. What is the class studying?
4. What is the teacher explaining?
5. What is Joseph doing?

6. Why is Luis raising his hand?
7. What is Sonia borrowing?
8. What is Henry doing?
9. Who is walking in late?
10. Why do you think she is late?

Role play

With a partner, write a conversation between two students. It's the first day of school. Introduce yourselves and find out some information about each other. Present your dialogue to the class.

2 Around the House

What chores do you have to do at
   home every week?
What do you enjoy doing?
What do you hate doing?
What chores does each person in
   your family do at home?
How do you relax at home?

Listen, Read and Say

Ted: Hi, John. This is Ted.
John: Hi, Ted. How are you doing?
Ted: Fine. Listen. I'm not doing anything right now. Is it alright to drop
       by for a while?
John: Well . . . we're pretty busy right now. I'm cleaning the basement
       and Joan is typing a report. How about coming over later?
Ted: Okay. How about 3:00?
John: Good. See you then. Bye.

Practice
Practice

Practice this model. Talk about the chores below.

> _____ **He's mopping the floor** _____ now.

1. he/mop the floor

2. they/cook dinner

3. I/vacuum

4. she/make the bed

5. they/do the laundry

6. I/pay the bills

Practice this model. Ask and answer questions.

> A: What _____ *is he* _____ doing?
> B: _____ *He's watching t.v.* _____ .

1. he/watch   2. she/write   3. I/read   4. they/play

5. I/bake   6. he/type   7. they/study   8. she/make

Ask and answer questions about these activities.

Partner Exercise

Student 1

What/they/do?
What are they doing?

1. What/they/do?
2. They/work/in the garden.
3. What/he/watch?
4. He/watch/a baseball game.
5. What/you/paint?
6. I/paint/living room.
7. What/he/do?
8. He/take/a nap.
9. What/she/do?
10. She/cut/lawn.
11. What/you/cook?
12. I/cook/fish.
13. What/she/do?
14. She/take/a bubble bath.

(FOLD HERE)

Student 2
Listen carefully and help Student 1 say the sentence correctly.

1. What are they doing?
2. They're working in the garden.
3. What is he watching?
4. He's watching a baseball game.
5. What are you painting?
6. I'm painting the living room.
7. What is he doing?
8. He's taking a nap.
9. What is she doing?
10. She's cutting the lawn.
11. What are you cooking?
12. I'm cooking fish.
13. What is she doing?
14. She's taking a bubble bath.

CONCEN **TRATION** *Cut out and play the Concentration Game on page 85. Match each picture with the correct problem.*

complete

Complete these sentences.

1. They ___'re studying___ for a test. (study)
2. He _____ a shower. (take)
3. I _____ the windows. (wash)
4. I _____ lunch. (make)
5. He _____ the grass. (cut)
6. He _____ his shirts. (iron)
7. She _____ the furniture. (dust)
8. I _____ the oven. (clean)
9. She _____ the laundry. (do)
10. She _____ the floor. (mop)

Interaction

Ask two students these questions about their typical weekend activities. Circle **Yes** *or* **No** *for each question on the chart below.*

ACTIVITY	STUDENT 1	STUDENT 2
1. Do you clean your house on the weekend?	Yes No	Yes No
2. Do you vacuum?	Yes No	Yes No
3. Do you work?	Yes No	Yes No
4. Do you watch tv?	Yes No	Yes No
5. Do you do the laundry?	Yes No	Yes No
6. Do you wash your car?	Yes No	Yes No
7. Do you do your homework?	Yes No	Yes No
8. Do you pay your bills?	Yes No	Yes No
9. Do you go food shopping?	Yes No	Yes No
10. Do you visit friends?	Yes No	Yes No

Talk about the backyard family scene. Where is each person in this family? What is each person doing? Write the new vocabulary on the picture.

Match this telephone conversation. Practice the sentences with a partner.

Hi. How are you doing?   Well, I'm working in the yard.

It's a beautiful day, isn't it?   Good, thanks.

Is it okay to drop by now?   Yes, we're all outside.

How about Dave? What's he   How about 5:00?
  doing?   Good. See you later.

What time is good for you?   He's waxing the car.

Okay, I'll see you then.

Role play

With another student, write a telephone conversation between two friends. Decide on a good time to stop by for a visit. Present your dialogue to the class.

9

3 Housing Problems

Discuss

What kinds of problems do you sometimes
   have in your apartment or house?
Who do you call to fix them?
How soon does someone come?
What can you do if the super will
   not fix the problem?

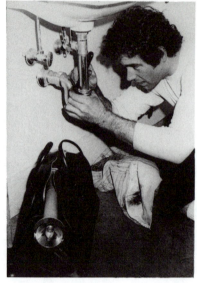

Listen, Read and Say

Super: Hello.
Mrs. Gomez: This is Mrs. Gomez, apartment 312. The ceiling in the living
   room is leaking.
Super: All right. I'll be up some time this week.
Mrs. Gomez: You need to come up right now. There's water all over the
   floor.
Super: That's a bad leak. I'll be there soon.

Practice Practice

Practice this model with the problems below.

The _____ *air conditioner* _____ isn't working.

1. air conditioner

2. oven

3. light switch

4. dishwasher

5. burner on my
   stove

6. refrigerator

7. radiator

8. outlet

10

Practice this model with the housing problems below.

> The _____*ceiling*_____ is _____*leaking*_____.

1. ceiling/leak

2. toilet/overflow

3. plaster/fall

4. radiator/leak

5. sink/overflow

6. faucet/drip

CONCEN TRATION **Cut out and play the Concentration Game on page 87. Match each picture with the correct sentence.**

Partner Exercise

Describe the problem in each apartment.

Student 1	**Student 2**
toilet/overflow The toilet is overflowing.	**Listen carefully and help Student 1 say the sentence correctly.**

Student 1		Student 2
1. toilet/overflow		1. The toilet is overflowing.
2. faucet/drip		2. The faucet is dripping.
3. light switch/not work		3. The light switch isn't working.
4. stove/not work		4. The stove isn't working.
5. radiator/leak		5. The radiator is leaking.
6. heat/not work	(FOLD HERE)	6. The heat isn't working.
7. sink/overflow		7. The sink is overflowing.
8. plaster/fall		8. The plaster is falling.
9. dishwasher/not work		9. The dishwasher isn't working.
10. air conditioner/not work		10. The air conditioner isn't working.
11. ceiling/leak		11. The ceiling is leaking.
12. one of the burners/not work		12. One of the burners isn't working.

11

Complete these conversations about the apartment problems in the pictures below.

some time today	tomorrow	this weekend
this afternoon	in a few days	as soon as I can

Super: Hello.
Tenant: This is Mr. Davis, apartment 14.
       The toilet is overflowing. _____.
Super: I'll be there _tomorrow._ _____.
Tenant: It's an emergency. You must come now.

Super: Hello.
Tenant: This is Mrs. Beltran, apartment 1A.
    _____.
Super: I'll be there _____.
Tenant: This can't wait. You must come immediately.

Super: Hello.
Tenant: This is Mrs. DeMarco, apartment 28.
    _____.
Super: I'll be there _____.
Tenant: We've waited three days already.

Super: Hello.
Tenant: This is Mr. Roberts, apartment B4.
    _____.
Super: I'll be there _____.
Tenant: You told me that yesterday, but you didn't come.

Interaction

Ask two students these questions about their houses or apartments. Then, fill in the information on the chart below.

Do you live in a house or in an apartment?
What are some of the problems in your house (or apartment)?

STUDENT	PLACE	PROBLEMS
	house apartment	
	house apartment	

Putting It Together

Talk about the problems in this apartment building. Write the new vocabulary on the picture.

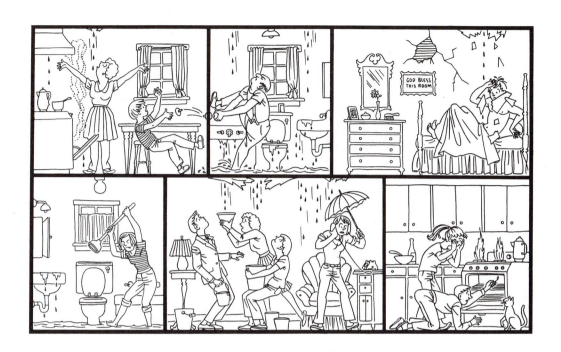

Match this conversation between a tenant and a super. Practice the sentences with a partner.

This is Mrs. Butler, Apartment 3.

The sink is leaking.

Tomorrow! I need you now.

Okay. What time this afternoon?

Good. I'll see you at 3:30.

Now? I'll come up this afternoon.

Of course. I'll see you then.

I'll fix it tomorrow.

Yes, Mrs. Butler. What's the problem?

At 3:30.

With another student, write a telephone conversation between a tenant and a super. There is a serious problem in your apartment. The super doesn't want to come right away. Present your dialogue to the class.

Role play

4 The Weekend

Discuss

Do you have any free time
on the weekend?
What do you like to do
on the weekend?
What are you going to do
this weekend?
Are you going to do
anything special?

Listen, Read and Say

Carmen: Would you like to come over on Saturday?
Angela: This weekend is out. My sister and her family are going to arrive
on Saturday. On Sunday we're going to visit my parents.
Carmen: Well, maybe we can get together next weekend.
Angela: Sounds good. I'll call you.

Practice
Practice

Practice this model with the activities below.

A: What are you going to do this weekend?
B: **_We're going to visit some friends_** .

1. We/visit some friends

2. I/look for a new tv

3. I/go to the park

4. We/pick up my mother at
the airport

5. We/have a party

6. I/go shopping

Practice this model with the activities below.

| A: What is he going to do this weekend?
 B: _____ **He's going to fix his car** _____. | A: What are they going to do this weekend?
 B: _____ **They're going to eat out** _____. |

1. He/fix his car

2. They/eat out

3. She/go to the mall

4. He/play soccer

5. She/stay home and watch tv

6. They/get together with some friends

Partner Exercise

Make statements about these future activities.

Student 1

I/listen to music
I'm going to listen to music.

1. I/listen to music
2. They/look for a used car

3. She/visit her parents
4. He/read
5. We/go to the library
6. I/sleep late
7. She/work
8. They/stay home
9. He/buy some clothes

10. We/go dancing

(FOLD HERE)

Student 2
Listen carefully and help Student 1 say the sentence correctly.

1. I'm going to listen to music.
2. They're going to look for a used car.
3. She's going to visit her parents.
4. He's going to read.
5. We're going to go to the library.
6. I'm going to sleep late.
7. She's going to work.
8. They're going to stay home.
9. He's going to buy some clothes.
10. We're going to go dancing.

Cut out and play the Concentration Game on page 87. Match each picture with the correct sentence.

complete

Complete these statements about next weekend.

1. I <u>'m going to stay</u> at home. (stay)
2. He _____ some friends on Sunday. (see)
3. They _____ downtown on Saturday. (go)
4. We _____ next Saturday. (eat out)
5. She _____ tennis next Sunday. (play)
6. I _____ camping next weekend. (go)
7. They _____ a new refrigerator this weekend. (buy)
8. She _____ her sister this Saturday. (visit)
9. We _____ a video Saturday night. (rent)
10. He _____ his son's bicycle Saturday morning. (fix)

Interaction

Ask another student these questions about his weekend plans. Check Yes or No for each activity. If the answer is Yes, ask questions with Where, What, When or Who. Fill in the information on the chart below.

Are you going to <u>*rent a movie*</u> this weekend?
<u>*What movie are you going to rent*</u> ?

QUESTION	YES	NO	MORE INFORMATION
1. rent a movie			
2. visit your family			
3. go shopping			
4. eat out			
5. visit some friends			
6. go to a party			
7. play soccer			
8. buy something for yourself			
9. go someplace special			
10. go to the movies			

<table>
<tr><td>Putting</td></tr>
<tr><td>It</td></tr>
<tr><td>Together</td></tr>
</table>

It's going to be a beautiful weekend. Lots of people are planning to go to the park. What is each person doing? What is going to happen to each person? Write the new vocabulary on the picture.

Discuss these questions.

1. Who is hiding behind a tree?
2. Why is the teenager hiding behind the tree?
3. What's Liz going to do after the boy steals her bicycle?
4. Why is the boat tipping?
5. What's going to happen to Andre and Marc?
6. What's going to happen to Kim?
7. What's going to happen to Martin's car?
8. What's Martin going to do after the ball hits his car?
9. Where are Bob and Lisa sitting?
10. What are Bob and Lisa going to do when they see the skunk?
11. What's the dog going to do?
12. What's Tom going to do after the dog takes the meat?

Role play

With another student, write a conversation between two friends. Talk about your weekend plans. Present your dialogue to the class.

5 Vacation Plans

Are you going to go on vacation soon?
Where are you going to go?
  How are you going to get there?
What are you going to do there?
  How long are you going to stay?

Listen, Read and Say

Laura: We're going to Florida next week.
Andrea: That's great! When are you going to leave?
Laura: On Saturday.
Andrea: What are you going to do there?
Laura: We're going to spend a few days at the beach and then we're going to go to Disney World.
Andrea: How long are you going to stay?
Laura: For a week.
Andrea: Well, have a good time.

Practice
Practice

Ask and answer questions about the pictures below with this model.

> What _____*is*_____ _____*he*_____ going to do in Florida?
> _____*He's going to go to Disney World.*_____.

1. he
   go to Disney World

2. you
   go swimming

3. they
   visit relatives

4. they
   take a boat
   in the Everglades

5. she
   lie in the sun
   and relax

6. you
   see the show
   at Sea World

Partner Exercise

Ask and answer questions about a vacation to Washington, D.C.

<table>
<tr><td>

Student 1

What/he/do?
What's he going to do?

1. What/he/do?
2. He/visit the monuments.

3. What/you/do?
4. I/take a tour of the White House.
5. What/they/do?
6. They/go to the National Zoo.

7. What/you/do?
8. We/see the rockets at the Smithsonian Institute.
9. What/she/do?
10. She/walk around the city.

</td><td>

(FOLD HERE)

</td><td>

Student 2

Listen carefully and help Student 1 say the sentence correctly.

1. What's he going to do?
2. He's going to visit the monuments.

3. What are you going to do?
4. I'm going to take a tour of the White House.
5. What are they going to do?
6. They are going to go to the National Zoo.

7. What are you going to do?
8. We are going to see the rockets at the Smithsonian Institute.
9. What is she going to do?
10. She's going to walk around the city.

</td></tr>
</table>

Practice this model with the vacation plans below.

Where _are Tony and Maria_ going to go? _They're going to go to Washington._
When ___are they___ going to leave? _They're going to leave next Friday._
How long ___are they___ going to stay? _They're going to stay for a week._
What ___are they___ going to do? _They're going to go sightseeing._

	WHERE	**WHEN**	**HOW LONG**	**WHAT**
Tony and Maria	Washington, D.C.	next Friday	for 1 week	go sightseeing
Ali	Florida	next week	for 10 days	go to Disney World
Fabio and Hilda	Yellowstone National Park	in two weeks	for 3 weeks	go camping
Sonia	San Francisco	this Saturday	for 2 weeks	see friends
Mr. and Mrs. Vargas	to their country	in July	for a month	visit their families

19

Complete these questions and answers about the chart.

1. Where _____*is*_____ Ali ____*going to go*____?
2. *He's going to go to Florida* _____.
3. When _____ Ali _____?
4. _____.
5. How long _____ Ali _____ in Florida?
6. _____.
7. What _____ he _____ in Florida?
8. _____.
9. Where _____ Mr. and Mrs. Vargas _____?
10. _____.
11. When _____ Mr. and Mrs. Vargas _____?
12. _____.
13. How long _____ Mr. and Mrs. Vargas _____?
14. _____.

Interaction

Ask two students these questions about their vacation plans. Fill in their answers on the chart below.

Where are you going to go on vacation?
When are you going to leave?
How long are you going to stay?
What are you going to do?

WHERE	WHEN	HOW LONG	WHAT

Luis and Olga are going to fly to New York for a short vacation. A friend is going to drive them to the airport. This is their schedule for their first day:

ACTIVITY	TIME
arrive at the airport	7:15
check their baggage	7:30
get on the plane	8:30
take off	8:45
land	11:00
rent a car	11:30
check into the hotel	12:30
unpack	1:00
go sightseeing	2:00
have dinner	6:00
see a show	8:00

Discuss these questions about Luis and Olga's vacation plans.

1. Who's going to take them to the airport?
2. What time are they going to arrive at the airport?
3. What are they going to do first?
4. When are they going to board the plane?
5. What time is the plane going to take off?
6. How long is the flight going to be?
7. When is the plane going to land?
8. What time are they going to check into the hotel?
9. What are they going to do at 2:00?
10. When are they going to see a show?

Role play

With another student, write a conversation between two friends talking about their vacation plans. Present your dialogue to the class.

6 Day Care

Discuss

Do any children in your family go to
   a preschool or a day-care center?
Why do parents send their children
   to day care?
How do you choose
   a good day-care center?

Listen, Read and Say

Clara: I'm looking for a day-care center for Marisa.
Marie: Jeffrey goes to Sundance. He's real happy there.
Clara: What's the program like?
Marie: The children play and make things. They also learn letters and numbers.
Clara: How about the teachers?
Marie: They're great. Jeffrey loves his teacher.
Clara: It sounds like a nice place. Can you drop your child off early?
Marie: Yes, they open at 7 a.m.
Clara: Thanks. I'll talk to the director and visit some classes.

Practice **Practice**

Talk about Jeffrey's schedule at the day-care center with this model.

He ___*gets to the day-care center early*___ every day.

1. get to the day-
   care center early
2. play with cars
   and trucks
3. learn letters
   and numbers
4. eat lunch

5. take a nap
6. paint
7. do arts and crafts
8. go outside

Practice
Practice

Talk about the children's activities at the day-care center with this model.

They _____ *sing songs* _____ every day.

1. sing songs   2. play games   3. talk about holidays   4. do puzzles

5. build with blocks   6. take walks   7. cut and paste pictures   8. dance

CONCEN **TRATION**   **Cut out and play the Concentration Game on page 89. Match each picture with the correct sentence.**

Partner Exercise

Make statements about the day-care center.

Student 1 The teacher/read stories The teacher reads stories.	**Student 2** *Listen carefully and help Student 1 say the sentence correctly.*
1. The teacher/read stories	1. The teacher reads stories.
2. They/talk about the weather	2. They talk about the weather.
3. The children/play house	3. The children play house.
4. The teacher/ help the students	4. The teacher helps the students.
5. She/go on field trips	5. She goes on field trips.
6. He/draw and paint	6. He draws and paints.
7. They/clean up	7. They clean up.
8. They/take naps	8. They take naps.
9. She/have a snack	9. She has a snack.
10. The children/play dress up	10. The children play dress up.

(FOLD HERE)

complete

Complete this description of a day-care center in the present tense.

At the nursery school, the teacher ____**comes**____ (come) in early and _____ (prepare) the activities for the day. The children _____ (arrive) at school at 8:30 in the morning. The teacher _____ (greet) the children and they _____ (sit) down in the circle. The teacher and the children _____ (talk) about the weather and the calendar. After that, the teacher _____ (send) the children to different activity centers in the room. Children _____ (play) in the housekeeping corner, the science corner, and the dress-up corner. Other children _____ (paint) at the easels. Some children _____ (do) puzzles and arts and crafts. The teacher _____ (walk) around the room and _____ (help) the children. Then, the children _____ (have) a snack. Later, the teacher _____ (play) the piano and the children _____ (sing) songs. After that, they usually _____ (go) outside and _____ (play) in the playground. Sometimes, the teacher _____ (take) the children for a walk. When they _____ (come) back inside, it _____ (be) lunch time. Some children _____ (go) home around 12:00. Other children _____ (stay) at school for the afternoon program.

Interaction

Ask two students these questions about child care. Fill in their answers on the chart below.

Do any children in your family go to a preschool, or to a day-care center?
How old are they?
Where do they go?
What hours do they attend?

CHILD AND AGE	PLACE	HOURS

This is a typical day-care center with activity centers. The children play in one activity center at a time. What items are in each area? What do the children do in each of these centers? Write new vocabulary on the picture below.

Match this conversation between a parent and a day-care center director. Then, practice the questions and answers with a partner.

Are the teachers certified?

How many children are in the class?

Does my child have to be toilet trained?

How much does your program cost?

Is there early morning drop off?

What are the hours?

No more than ten.

From 9:00 to 5:00.

Yes, they have early childhood certification.

Yes, you can bring your child any time after 7:00 a.m.

No, the aide changes diapers.

It's $300 a month.

Role play

With another student, write a conversation between a parent and a school director. Ask about the program. Discuss time, activities, teachers, size of class, cost, and other information about the school. Present your dialogue to the class.

7 School

Discuss

What was your favorite subject
  in high school?
What subjects do students study
  in junior high and in high school
  in the United States?
What clubs, sports, and other activities are
  available for students after school?

Listen, Read and Say

Kim:	How's your schedule?
Megan:	It's okay. Who do you have for biology?
Kim:	Mrs. Brown.
Megan:	Oh! She's hard! And she gives a lot of homework.
Kim:	How about you?
Megan:	I have Mr. Campos.
Kim:	He's great, but be careful. He gives surprise quizzes.
Megan:	Thanks for telling me. See you at lunch.

Practice
 Practice

Practice this model with the courses below.

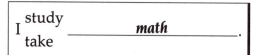

I study _____ *math* _____ .
 take

He studies _____ *chemistry* _____ .
 takes

$75\% \text{ of } 60 = 45$

H_2O

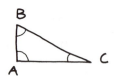

1. I/math   2. he/chemistry   3. she/geometry   4. I/biology

$2(4x + 7y) = 62$

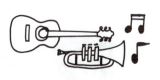

5. they/algebra   6. she/social studies   7. I/English   8. we/music

Practice this model with the courses below.

A: Do ___*you*___ take ___*geography*___ ?

B: Yes, ___*I*___ do.

No, ___*I*___ don't.

A: Does ___*he*___ take ___*Spanish*___ ?

B: Yes, ___*he*___ does.

No, ___*he*___ doesn't.

1. you/geography   2. he/Spanish   3. they/French   4. she/music

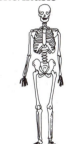

5. they/psychology   6. you/band   7. she/art   8. he/health

Ask and answer questions about these courses.

Student 1	Student 2
he/study/geometry?	**Listen carefully and help Student 1 say the sentence correctly.**
Does he study geometry?	

Student 1

1. she/study/geometry?
2. Yes
3. he/take/physical education?

4. Yes
5. they/study/algebra?
6. No
7. you/take/art?
8. Yes
9. she/study/accounting?
10. No
11. they/take/word processing?
12. Yes
13. he/study/Latin?
14. No

(FOLD HERE)

Student 2

1. Does she study geometry?
2. Yes, she does.
3. Does he take physical education?
4. Yes, he does.
5. Do they study algebra?
6. No, they don't.
7. Do you take art?
8. Yes, I do.
9. Does she study accounting?
10. No, she doesn't.
11. Do they take word processing?
12. Yes, they do.
13. Does he study Latin?
14. No, he doesn't.

27

Complete these conversations with Do or Does. Write the answer.

1. __*Does*__ he take chemistry?   Yes, __*he*__ __*does*__.
2. _____ she belong to the computer club?   Yes, _____ _____.
3. _____ you sing in the chorus?   No, _____ _____.
4. _____ they study auto mechanics?   Yes, _____ _____.
5. _____ she take woodworking?   Yes, _____ _____.
6. _____ you play in the school band?   Yes, _____ _____.
7. _____ he play on the soccer team?   No, _____ _____.
8. _____ they use the school library?   Yes, _____ _____.
9. _____ you write for the school newspaper?   No, _____ _____.
10. _____ she take driver education?   Yes, _____ _____.

Interaction

Ask these questions to a student who has a relative in high school. Check Yes or No for each question. If the answer is Yes, ask for more information. Fill in the information on the chart below.

Does she _____*take math*_____?
_____*Which math does she take*_____?

QUESTION	YES	NO	MORE INFORMATION
1. take math?			
2. study science?			
3. play in the school band?			
4. belong to any clubs?			
5. take an elective?			
6. take any honors courses?			
7. play on a school team?			
8. study a second language?			

Talk about this high school schedule. What courses does this student take? Is this schedule similar to a high school schedule in your country?

High School Schedule
Student: Megan Sanders, 10th Grade   Homeroom 126

PERIOD	COURSE	TEACHER	ROOM
1	Algebra	Campos	126
2	Spanish 3	Ziobro	318
3	Computers	Gerson	307
4	Physical Education	Barba	Gym 2
5	Lunch		Cafeteria
6	English	Marino	120
7	Geography	Young	202
8	Chorus	King	311
9	Biology	Tama	244

1. What grade is Megan in?
2. How many periods does she have in a day?
3. Who does she have for algebra?
4. What language does she study?
5. What period does she take Spanish?
6. What does Megan study third period?
7. Does she take physical education?
8. Which period does she have lunch?
9. When does she have English?
10. Where does she have chorus?
11. Which science does she take?
12. Does she have a study period?

Role play

With another student, write a conversation between two students. Talk about your school schedules, courses and teachers. Present your dialogue to the class.

8 Family

Discuss

Do you have any family
in the United States?
Where do they live?
How often do you see them?

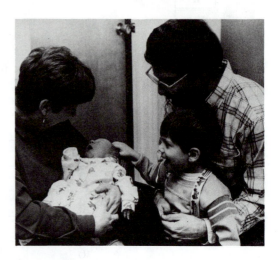

Listen, Read and Say

Lizzy: I'm going to visit my brother next week.
Adam: Your brother! You have a brother? Where does he live?
Lizzy: Peter lives in Michigan.
Adam: Is he married?
Lizzy: Yes. And he has two kids.
Adam: What does he do?
Lizzy: He's an engineer.
Adam: How often do you see him?
Lizzy: Not often, only once a year.
Adam: Well, have a good time.

Practice this model with the people and states below.

A: Where does _____*he*_____ live?	A: Where do _____*they*_____ live?
B: _____*He lives in California.*_____.	B: _____*They live in Arizona.*_____.

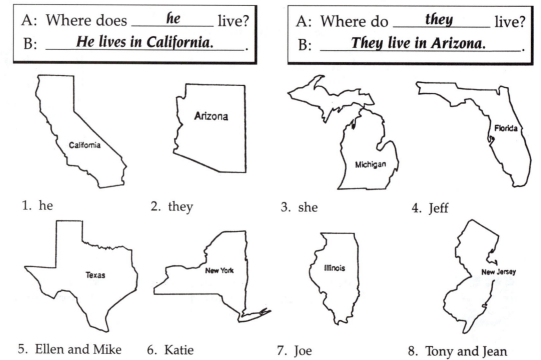

1. he   2. they   3. she   4. Jeff

5. Ellen and Mike   6. Katie   7. Joe   8. Tony and Jean

Practice this model. Talk about Adam's brother, sister and parents.

A: Where ___*does Robert*___ live?	B: ___*He lives in New Mexico.*___
A: What ___*does he*___ do?	B: ___*He's a police officer.*___
A: How often ___*do you see him*___ ?	B: ___*I see him twice a year.*___

ADAM'S FAMILY	WHERE/LIVE?	WHAT/DO?	HOW OFTEN/SEE?
brother **Robert**	New Mexico	police officer	twice a year
brother **Arnold**	Pennsylvania	computer analyst	once a month
sister **Clara**	California	x-ray technician	once a year
parents	Massachusetts	retired/nurse	every other month

Partner Exercise

Ask and answer questions about Sam.

Student 1	Student 2
Where/Sam/live?	**Listen carefully and help Student 1 say the sentence correctly.**
Where does Sam live?	

Student 1	Student 2
1. Where/Sam/live?	1. Where does Sam live?
2. He/live/Miami	2. He lives in Miami.
3. he/married?	3. Is he married?
4. Yes	4. Yes, he is.
5. What/he/do?	5. What does he do?
6. car salesman	6. He's a car salesman.
7. How many children/he/have?	7. How many children does he have?
8. four	8. He has four.
9. How often/you/see him?	9. How often do you see him?
10. once a month	10. I see him once a month.

(FOLD HERE)

31

complete

Complete these dialogues.

A: I'm going to visit my sister this weekend.

B: Your sister! Where ____*does*____ she ____*live*____ (live)?

A: In Chicago.

B: Is she married?

A: Yes, she _____ (be). And she _____ (have) two children.

B: What _____ she _____ (do)?

A: She _____ (be) a real estate agent.

B: How often _____ you _____ (see) her?

A: About two or three times a year.

A: I'm going to visit my parents next week.

B: Where _____ they _____ (live)?

A: In Dallas

B: Are they retired?

A: No. My mother _____ (be) a secretary and my father _____ (be) an accountant.

B: How often _____ you _____ (visit) them?

A: I _____ (fly) to Dallas once a year and they _____ (drive) here once a year.

Interaction

Ask two students these questions about one of their brothers, sisters, or their parent(s). Fill in the information on the chart below.

QUESTION	STUDENT 1	STUDENT 2
Do you have any relatives in the U.S.?		
Where _____ _____ live?		
Is _____ married?		
How many children _____ _____ have?		
What _____ _____ do?		
How often do you see _____?		

This is a map of the United States. What state do you live in? Do any of your family members live in the United States? Tell the class which states they live in. Discuss these questions about family members who live in other states.

What state and city does she live in? How far is it from here? How long does it take to get there? How often do you visit her? How often do you call her?

Role play

With another student, write a conversation between two friends. Talk about a family member or friend who lives in another state. Tell about her family and her job. Explain how often you see her. Present your conversation to the class.

9 Transportation

Discuss

What kind of public transportation
   is in your area?
How do you get to school?
When do you take the bus?
When do you take the train?
Do you have a schedule for the
   train or bus in your area?

Listen, Read and Say

Jack: The concert is at 8:00.
Tina: There's a bus at 6:30 and another at 7:15.
Jack: When does the 7:15 get there?
Tina: At 7:50.
Jack: That's cutting it too close. Let's take the 6:30.

Practice **Practice**

Look at the schedule and practice this model about the trains below.

A: When does the _____ **6:06** _____ from _____ **Fanwood** _____ arrive in _____ **New York** _____?
B: It arrives at _____ **7:02** _____.

Fanwood	Westfield	Cranford	Roselle Park	Newark	R F	New York
A.M.	A.M.	A.M.	A.M.	A.M.		A.M.
5.33	5.37	5.42	5.47	6.02		6.23
6.06	6.11	6.17	6.22	6.37		7.02
6.37	6.42	6.47	6.52	7.06		7.27
—	6.59	7.04	—	7.21		7.45
7.10	—	—	7.21	7.35		7.59
—	7.20	—	—	7.41		8.01
—	—	7.29	7.34	7.48		8.11
7.33	7.38	7.43	—	8.02		8.23
7.43	7.48	7.54	7.59	8.13		8.35
—	8.03	—	—	8.24		A8.50
8.14	8.19	8.24	8.29	8.43		9.05
9.00	9.05	9.10	9.17	9.31		9.51
10.20	10.25	10.30	10.35	10.50		11.11

Then hourly service until

Fanwood	Westfield	Cranford	Roselle Park	Newark	R F	New York
P.M.	P.M.	P.M.	P.M.	P.M.		P.M.
4.18	4.23	4.29	4.34	4.50		5.10
5.19	5.24	5.31	5.36	5.50		6.12
5.44	5.49	5.54	5.59	6.14		6.42
6.22	6.26	6.31	—	6.48		7.21
6.48	6.53	6.58	7.03	7.18		7.41
7.48	7.53	7.58	8.03	8.18		8.40
8.48	8.53	8.58	9.03	9.18		9.40
9.48	9.53	9.58	10.03	10.18		10.40
11.15	11.20	11.25	11.30	11.45		12.10
12.15	12.20	12.25	12.30	12.45		1.10

	TIME	FROM	ARRIVE IN
1.	6:06 am	Fanwood	New York
2.	9:00 am	Fanwood	Westfield
3.	10:25 am	Westfield	New York
4.	5:49 pm	Westfield	Newark
5.	6:31 pm	Cranford	New York
6.	7:58 pm	Cranford	Newark
7.	11:30 pm	Roselle Park	New York

You live in Fanwood. Read each situation, study the schedule, and decide which train to catch. Use this model.

A: There's a train at ___**10:20**___ and another at ___**11:20**___.
B: Let's take the ___**11:20**___.

Fanwood	Westfield	Cranford	Roselle Park	Newark	R F	New York
Monday through Friday						
A.M.	A.M.	A.M.	A.M.	A.M.		A.M.
5.33	5.37	5.42	5.47	6.02		6.23
6.06	6.11	6.17	6.22	6.37		7.02
6.37	6.42	6.47	6.52	7.06		7.27
—	6.59	7.04	—	7.21		7.45
7.10	—	—	7.21	7.35		7.59
—	7.20	—	—	7.41		8.01
—	—	7.29	7.34	7.48		8.11
7.33	7.38	7.43	—	8.02		8.23
7.43	7.48	7.54	7.59	8.13		8.35
—	8.03	—	—	8.24		A8.50
8.14	8.19	8.24	8.29	8.43		9.05
9.00	9.05	9.10	9.17	9.31		9.51
10.20	10.25	10.30	10.35	10.50		11.11
Then hourly service until						
P.M.	P.M.	P.M.	P.M.	P.M.		P.M.
4.18	4.23	4.29	4.34	4.50		5.10
5.19	5.24	5.31	5.36	5.50		6.12
5.44	5.49	5.54	5.59	6.14		6.42
6.22	6.26	6.31	—	6.48		7.21
6.48	6.53	6.58	7.03	7.18		7.41
7.48	7.53	7.58	8.03	8.18		8.40
8.48	8.53	8.58	9.03	9.18		9.40
9.48	9.53	9.58	10.03	10.18		10.40
11.15	11.20	11.25	11.30	11.45		12.10
12.15	12.20	12.25	12.30	12.45		1.10
Saturday and Presidents' Day						
A.M.	A.M.	A.M.	A.M.	A.M.		A.M.
12.15	12.20	12.25	12.30	12.45		1.10
5.45	5.50	5.55	6.00	6.15		6.43
7.20	7.25	7.30	7.35	7.50		8.17
8.20	8.25	8.30	8.35	8.50		9.17
9.20	9.25	9.30	9.35	9.50		10.17
Then hourly service until						
P.M.	P.M.	P.M.	P.M.	P.M.		P.M.
4.20	4.25	4.30	4.35	4.50		5.17
5.20	5.25	5.30	5.35	5.50		6.17
6.20	6.25	6.30	6.35	6.50		7.17
7.20	7.25	7.30	7.35	7.50		8.17
8.20	8.25	8.30	8.35	8.50		9.17
9.20	9.25	9.30	9.35	9.50		10.17
10.20	10.25	10.30	10.35	10.50		11.17
11.20	11.25	11.30	11.35	11.50		12.17
Sunday - Major Holidays except Presidents' Day						
A.M.	A.M.	A.M.	A.M.	A.M.		A.M.
5.45	5.50	5.55	6.00	6.15		6.43
8.20	8.25	8.30	8.35	8.50		9.17
10.20	10.25	10.30	10.35	10.50		11.17
Then hourly service until						
P.M.	P.M.	P.M.	P.M.	P.M.		P.M.
4.20	4.25	4.30	4.35	4.50		5.17
5.20	5.25	5.30	5.35	5.50		6.17
6.20	6.25	6.30	6.35	6.50		7.17
7.20	7.25	7.30	7.35	7.50		8.17
8.20	8.25	8.30	8.35	8.50		9.17
9.20	9.25	9.30	9.35	9.50		10.17
11.20	11.25	11.30	11.35	11.50		12.17

1. You have a job interview in New York at 1:00 p.m.

2. You have a doctor's appointment in Westfield at 11:00 a.m.

3. Your friends are giving a party in Cranford on Saturday night. It begins at 8:00 p.m.

4. Your appointment is in Roselle Park at 3:00 p.m.

5. You're going shopping. You want to be in Westfield around 12:00 p.m.

6. You're going to meet a friend in front of the post office in Cranford. You want to be there at 12:00 p.m.

7. You want to see the new exhibit at the art museum in New York on Sunday. You want to be there by 1:00 p.m.

8. The movie in Newark starts at 7:20 p.m.

9. You're going to visit your friend in the hospital in Newark. The visiting hours are from 7:00 to 9:00 p.m.

10. The baseball game in New York begins at 4:00 p.m. on Sunday.

Practice this model. How does each person below get to school?

A: How __*does Ali*__ get to school?	B: ____*He rides his bicycle.*____
A: What time __*does he*__ leave?	B: ____*He leaves at 7:15.*____
A: What time __*does he*__ get there?	B: ____*He gets there at 7:30.*____
A: How long does it take?	B: It takes ____*15 minutes.*____

1. Ali
7:15–7:30

2. David
8:00–8:20

3. Angela
7:30–8:15

4. Sonia
8:00–8:40

5. Pierre
7:45–8:15

6. Carmen
7:40–8:10

complete

Answer these questions about yourself.

1. How do you get to school?   _____

2. What time do you leave?   _____

3. What time do you arrive?   _____

4. How long does it take?   _____

Interaction

Ask three students these questions about getting to school. Fill in their information on the chart below.

QUESTIONS	STUDENT 1	STUDENT 2	STUDENT 3
How do you get to school?			
What time do you leave your house?			
What time do you arrive at school?			
How long does it take you?			

Fritz takes the bus to school every day. Talk about his commute. Write the new vocabulary on the picture.

Discuss these questions.

1. Where does Fritz catch the bus?
2. What time does he get on the bus?
3. Which bus does he take?
4. Is the bus crowded?
5. Does he usually get a seat or stand?
6. How much is the fare?
7. Can he give the bus driver two dollar bills?
8. Where does he get off the bus?
9. What time does the bus arrive?
10. How long does the bus ride take?

Role play

With another student, write a conversation between two friends. Describe your commute to school. Talk about the time, the traffic, and the cost. Present your dialogue to the class.

10 Money

Discuss

When do you borrow money from friends?
When do you borrow money from family?
Did you ever lend someone money?
How much? Why?

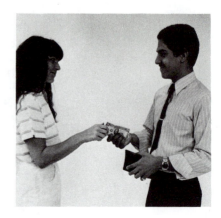

Listen, Read and Say

Patty: Luis, I want to get lunch, but I don't have money with me. Can you lend me five dollars?

Luis: Sure, here.

Patty: Thanks a lot. I'll pay you back tomorrow.

Practice **Practice**

Practice both models with each situation below.

I want to _____ *get lunch* _____.
Can I borrow $_____ *10.00* _____?

I want to _____ *get lunch* _____.
Can you lend me $_____ *10.00* _____?

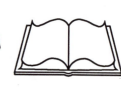

1. get lunch
   $10.00

2. get a sandwich
   $5.00

3. buy this sweater
   $30.00

4. get this book
   $12.00

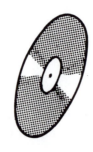

5. get some gas
   $20.00

6. buy this CD
   $15.00

7. get a soda
   $1.00

8. get two tickets for
   the concert $40.00

38

Complete these sentences with borrow or lend and give a reason.

1. Can you ____lend____ me $4.00?   I want to ____rent a video____

2. Can I _____ $25.00?   I want to _____

3. Can I _____ a dollar?   I need to _____

4. Can you _____ me $10.00?   I want to _____

5. Can I _____ $20.00?   I need to _____

Practice both models with the amounts and times below.

| Can I borrow $_____.25_____? | Can you lend me $_____.25_____? |
| I'll pay you back ____tomorrow____. | I'll pay you back ____tomorrow____. |

1. tomorrow   2. on Monday   3. next week

4. this weekend   5. on Friday   6. later

Partner Exercise

Ask a friend to lend you some money.

Student 1

lend/$15 on Friday?
Can you lend me $15?
I'll pay you back on Friday.

1. lend/$15.00?
   on Friday
2. borrow/$20.00?
   tomorrow
3. borrow/$5.00?
   next week
4. lend/$10.00?
   Tuesday
5. borrow/$50?
   next month
6. lend/$1.00?
   tomorrow

(FOLD HERE)

Student 2
***Listen carefully and help Student 1
say the sentence correctly.***

1. Can you lend me $15.00?
   I'll pay you back on Friday.
2. Can I borrow $20.00?
   I'll pay you back tomorrow.
3. Can I borrow $5.00?
   I'll pay you back next week.
4. Can you lend me $10.00?
   I'll pay you back on Tuesday.
5. Can I borrow $50.00?
   I'll pay you back next month.
6. Can you lend me $1.00?
   I'll pay you back tomorrow.

Cut out and play the Concentration Game on page 91. Match each picture with the correct sentence.

Complete

Complete these conversations. Use the expressions from the box below.

Sorry, I only have $_____.	Sorry, I'm broke.
Sorry, I don't have any money with me.	Sorry, I have to go shopping
Sorry, I don't have any change.	later.
Sorry, I don't get paid until _____.	Sure, here.

1. A: I ___*have to*___ make a phone call.

   Can I ___*borrow a quarter*___?

   B: Sorry, ___*I don't have any change*___.

2. A: I _____ get some gas.

   Can you _____?

   B: Sure, _____.

3. A: I _____ buy my textbook today.

   Can you _____?

   B: Sorry, _____.

4. A: I _____ buy this CD, but I don't have enough money with me.

   Can I _____?

   B: Sorry, _____.

5. A: I need to _____.

   Can you _____?

   B: Sorry, _____.

Ask three students these questions about their weekly expenses. Fill in their answers on the chart below.

How much do you spend on _____ a week?

Interaction

TRANSPORTATION	FOOD	RECREATION

Lamont and Alisha Hanson take home $2,500 a month. They have two children. Look carefully at their monthly budget, then discuss the questions.

Savings	$ 150
Rent	800
Electric and Gas	60
Heat	60
Telephone	70
Car loan payment	250
Clothing	100
Medical	60
Recreation	100
Food	400
Vacation	100
Piano Lessons	40
Miscellaneous	100
Gas	60
Repairs	50
Insurance	100
Total	$2500

1. How much is Lamont's and Alisha's take home pay?
2. How much do they save each month?
3. How much do Lamont and Alisha spend on _____?
4. How much do they pay for _____?
5. Do they have any loans? Is so, for what?
6. What are some miscellaneous expenses?
7. What are their biggest expenses?
8. What expenses seem high or low?
9. Do you have any expenses that are not included in their budget?
10. What expenses do Alisha and Lamont have that you do not have?

Role play

With another student, write a conversation between two friends or relatives. Ask to borrow some money and explain the reason. Present your dialogue to the class.

11 Deli

What's your favorite deli? Why?
What kind of deli food do you
  usually buy?
Do you ever stop at a deli
  and pick up a sandwich?
What kind?

Listen, Read and Say

Clerk: Next! Number 57!
Paula: Here! How much is the ham?
Clerk: It's $8.00 a pound.
Paula: I'll take a half a pound. And a pound of potato salad, please.
Clerk: That's $6.00.

Measurements

16 ounces = 1 pound
16 oz. = 1 lb.

8 ounces = 1/2 pound
8 oz. = 1/2 lb.

4 ounces = 1/4 pound
4 oz. = 1/4 lb.

Practice
Practice

Practice this model with the deli items below.

A: How much is the _____ *ham* _____?
B: $_____ *8.00* _____ a pound.

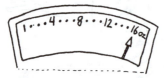
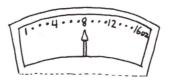
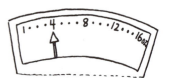

1. ham   2. turkey breast   3. salami   4. roast beef

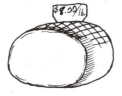

5. American cheese   6. Swiss cheese   7. cole slaw   8. potato salad

42

Practice these expressions with the teacher.

1/2 lb.	= (a) half of a pound *or* a half pound
1/4 lb.	= a quarter of a pound *or* a quarter pound
3/4 lb.	= three quarters of a pound
1 lb.	= one pound
1 1/2 lbs.	= a pound and a half
2 1/2 lbs.	= two and a half pounds

Practice these models with each amount below.

I'd like ____**a pound**____ of ham.

I'll take ____**a pound**____ of swiss cheese.

Please give me ____**a pound**____ of potato salad.

Let me have ____**a pound**____ of turkey.

1. 1 lb.   2. 2 lbs.   3. 1/2 lb.   4. 1/4 lb.

5. 3/4 lb.   6. 2 1/2 lbs.   7. 4 lbs.   8. 1 1/2 lbs.

CONCEN TRATION

Cut out and play the Concentration Game on page 93. Match the amount and the correct expression.

Partner Exercise

Give the order to the deli clerk.

Student 1	**Student 2**
1/4 lb. salami	*Listen carefully and help Student 1 say the sentence correctly.*
I'd like a quarter of a pound of salami.	

Student 1	Student 2
1. 1/2 lb./roast beef	1. I'd like a half pound of roast beef.
2. 1/4 lb./salami	2. I'd like a quarter of a pound of salami.
3. 3 lbs./potato salad	3. I'd like three pounds of potato salad.
4. 1 lb./American cheese	4. I'd like a pound of American cheese.
5. 3/4 lb./ham	5. I'd like three quarters of a pound of ham.
6. 2 lbs./cole slaw	6. I'd like two pounds of cole slaw.
7. 1 1/2 lbs./ turkey	7. I'd like a pound and a half of turkey.
8. 1/2 lb./Swiss cheese	8. I'd like a half pound of Swiss cheese.
9. 2 lbs./macaroni salad	9. I'd like two pounds of macaroni salad.

(FOLD HERE)

43

Write the price for each item.

1. A pound of ham is $8.00. How much is 1/2 lb.?   _**$4.00**_

2. A pound of roast beef is $10.00. How much is 1/4 lb.?   _____

3. A pound of potato salad is $1.39. How much is 2 lbs.?   _____

4. A pound of salami is $6.00. How much is 3/4 lb.?   _____

5. A pound of tuna salad is $7.00. How much is 1 1/2 lbs.?   _____

6. A pound of American cheese is $5.00. How much is 1/2 lb.?   _____

7. A pound of Swiss cheese is $8.00. How much is 1/4 lb.?   _____

Complete these conversations.

1. How much _____**is**_____ the ham? $9.00 a pound.
   **Let me have** two pounds.   That's _**$18.00**___.

2. How much _____ the cole slaw? $1.50 a pound.
   _____ three pounds.   That's $_____.

3. How much _____ the macaroni salad? $2.00 a pound.
   _____ a half a pound.   That's $_____.

4. How much _____ the chicken salad? $8.00 a pound.
   _____ 3/4 of a pound.   That's $_____.

5. How much _____ the roast beef? $10.00 a pound.
   _____ 1/4 pound.   That's $_____.

Interaction

Complete this chart. Write the cost of each item.

ITEM	PRICE PER POUND	WEIGHT	COST
Ham	$9.00	.50 lb.	_**$4.50**_
Turkey	$8.00	.25 lb.	
Potato salad	$2.00	1.5 lbs.	
Cole slaw	$1.50	2.5 lbs.	
Swiss cheese	$4.00	.75 lb.	

44

Plan a luncheon for your class. You're going to have sandwiches and salads. Look at the deli counter and decide the menu.

What do we need?
How many pounds do we need?
How much is the _____?
What's the total cost?

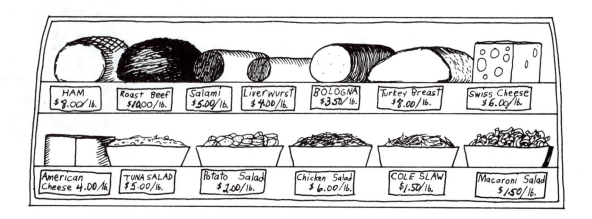

ITEM	HOW MANY POUNDS	PRICE PER POUND	TOTAL

With a partner, write a conversation between a customer and a deli clerk. Order some deli items for your family. Present the dialogue to the class.

Role play

12 Lunch

How often do you eat out for lunch?
What kind of food do you like for lunch?
Where do you eat out?

Listen, Read and Say

Waitress:	Good afternoon. Are you ready to order?
Joseph:	Yes, please. I'd like the special.
Waitress:	That comes with potatoes and a salad. What kind of potato would you like?
Joseph:	French fries.
Waitress:	And what kind of dressing would you like?
Joseph:	Italian, please.
Waitress:	Anything to drink?
Joseph:	Coffee.

Practice **Practice**

Practice this model with the menu items below.

I'd like _____ *a hamburger* _____.

1. a hamburger

2. a hot dog
   a frankfurter

3. a ham sandwich

4. a tuna fish sandwich

5. a turkey club

6. the fried fish

7. a chef's salad

8. a grilled cheese with bacon

Practice this model with the menu items below.

A: What kind of ___*potato*___ would you like?
B: I'd like ___*french fries*___, please.

potato   french fries   mashed   baked

salad dressing   Italian   French   Thousand Island   blue cheese

vegetable   peas   corn   carrots   green beans

soup   vegetable   chicken noodle   onion   split pea

A: How would you like your hamburger?
B: ___*Rare*___, please.

rare   medium rare   medium   well done

Partner Exercise

Ask and answer questions about these lunch orders

Student 1	Student 2
What kind/potato?	*Listen carefully and help Student 1 say the sentence correctly.*
What kind of potato would you like?	

Student 1

1. What kind/potato?
2. baked
3. What kind/vegetable?

4. carrots
5. What kind/dressing?
6. French
7. What kind/soup?
8. onion
9. What kind/dressing?
10. Italian
11. What kind/vegetable?

12. green beans

(FOLD HERE)

Student 2

1. What kind of potato would you like?
2. I'd like baked, please.
3. What kind of vegetable would you like?
4. I'd like carrots, please.
5. What kind of dressing would you like?
6. I'd like French, please.
7. What kind of soup would you like?
8. I'd like onion, please.
9. What kind of dressing would you like?
10. I'd like Italian, please.
11. What kind of vegetable would you like?
12. I'd like green beans, please.

Interaction

Ask three students these questions about a restaurant they like. Fill in their answers on the chart below.

Where do you eat out?
What do you usually order?
How much does a meal usually cost?
How much do you leave for a tip?

RESTAURANT AND LOCATION	ORDER	COST	TIP

Read the menu carefully. Take a lunch order from two students. Write each order on a check. How much should they leave for a tip?

Barbara's Cafe

Tuna Melt Special
Open-faced tuna on rye with
melted cheese and tomato
French Fries
Pudding or Ice Cream
Beverage
$5.90

Grilled Reuben Special
Corned beef, saurkraut,
swiss cheese and
russian dressing on rye
French Fries
Cole Slaw
Beverage
$6.95

Burger Special
6 oz. Cheeseburger
lettuce and tomato
French Fries
Pudding or Ice Cream
Beverage
$6.25

Sandwiches

Ham	4.50
Ham and Cheese	4.90
Turkey	5.25
Roast Beef	5.00
Corned Beef	5.25
Tuna Salad	4.50
Chicken Salad	4.90
Grilled Cheese	3.25

Clubs

Turkey and Bacon	6.50
Bacon, Lettuce and Tomato	5.90
Ham, Cheese and Bacon	6.00
Ham and Turkey	6.75

Salads

Chef Salad	7.25
Garden Salad	3.25
Tuna Salad Platter	6.10

From the Grill

Hamburger	4.25
Hamburger Deluxe	5.50
Cheeseburger	4.75
Cheeseburger Deluxe	6.00
Hot Dog	2.50

Beverages

Soda	1.25
Coffee or Tea	.80
Hot Chocolate	1.00
Milk	1.00
Chocolate Milk	1.10

Desserts

Rice Pudding	1.25
Cakes	1.90
Pies	1.90
Ice Cream	1.50
Sundaes	2.90

Role play

With another student, write a conversation between a waitress and a customer. Ask about the specials and order lunch. Present your dialogue to the class.

13 Shopping

Discuss

Did you ever return an item to a store?
What was the reason?
Did you exchange it or get a refund?
Did the clerk ask you any questions?

Listen, Read and Say

Clerk: Can I help you?
Jenny: I bought this sweater for my husband, but it's too small.
Clerk: Do you have the receipt?
Jenny: Yes, here it is.

Practice
Practice

Practice this model with the articles of clothing below.

I bought this ____*dress*____ for my ____*daughter*____,
but it's too ____*large*____.

1. daughter
   large

2. husband
   small

3. mother
   loose

4. brother
   tight

5. sister
   long

6. son
   short

Practice this model with the articles of clothing below.

I bought these _____ **pants** _____ for my _____ **son** _____,
but they're too _____ **short** _____.

1. son
   short

2. wife
   tight

3. husband
   loose

4. daughter
   long

5. brother
   big

6. sister
   small

 Partner Exercise

Explain the problem with each item of clothing.

Student 1	**Student 2**
	Listen carefully and help Student 1 say the sentence correctly.

jeans/son tight
I bought these jeans for my son, but they're too tight.

Student 1

1. jeans/son
   tight
2. blouse/daughter
   large
3. boots/brother
   tight
4. coat/mother
   small
5. jacket/son
   loose
6. pajamas/husband
   big
7. sweater/sister
   small

(FOLD HERE)

Student 2

1. I bought these jeans for my son, but they're too tight.
2. I bought this blouse for my daughter, but it's too large.
3. I bought these boots for my brother, but they're too tight.
4. I bought this coat for my mother, but it's too small.
5. I bought this jacket for my son, but it's too loose.
6. I bought these pajamas for my husband, but they're too big.
7. I bought this sweater for my sister, but it's too small.

51

Practice this model with the problems below.

I bought this _____dress_____ yesterday,
but ___the collar is stained___.
I'd like to return it.

I bought these _pajamas_ yesterday,
but ___the pocket is ripped___.
I'd like to exchange them.

1. the collar is stained

2. the pocket is ripped

3. the button is missing

4. the seam is ripped

5. the sleeve is stained

6. the zipper is broken

Cut out and play the Concentration Game on page 93. Match each picture with the correct sentence.

Interaction

Ask three students these questions about their shopping experiences. Fill in their answers on the chart below. Circle exchange or refund.

Did you ever return something to a store? What did you return?
What was the problem?
Did you exchange it or get a refund?

ITEM	PROBLEM	EXCHANGE/REFUND	
		exchange	refund
		exchange	refund

These customers are returning items in a clothing store. What kind of clothing does this store sell? What is each person returning? What's wrong with it? What's on sale at this store? What's the discount? Write the new vocabulary words on the picture.

Match this conversation between a clerk and a customer in a clothing store. Practice it with a partner.

Can I help you?

What's the problem?

Do you have a receipt?

Would you like to exchange them or get a refund?

Okay, pick out something else you'd like.

The zipper is broken

Thanks, I'll look around.

Yes, I'd like to return these pants.

Yes, here it is.

I'd like to exchange them.

Role play

With another student, write a conversation between a clerk and a customer. The customer is returning an article of clothing to a store. Explain the problem and ask for a refund or exchange the item. Present your dialogue to the class.

14 Work Experience

Discuss

Where do you work now?
What do you do?
What did you do in your country?
What kind of job would you like
  in the future?

Listen, Read and Say

Interviewer: Are you working?
 Ms. Young: I work in a warehouse. I'm a hi-lo operator.
Interviewer: Tell me about your previous experience.
 Ms. Young: I worked in a factory. I was a machine operator.

Practice this model with these occupations.

| ___*I*___ was a/an ___*typist*___. | ___*They*___ were ___*security guard*___s. |

1. I/typist

2. they/security guards

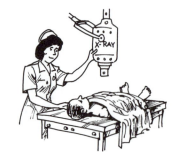

3. she/x-ray technician

4. I/hi-lo operator

5. he/electrician

6. they/data entry clerks

Practice this model with these occupations.

> _____ *I* _____ worked in a/an _____ *a plastic factory* _____ from _____ *1989* _____ to _____ *1991* _____.
> _____ *I* _____ was a/an _____ *a machine operator* _____.

1. I/plastics factory
   1989–1991
   machine operator

2. he/drug company
   1986–1993
   shipping clerk

3. he/insurance company
   1985–1991
   bookkeeper

4. she/hospital
   1984–1992
   nurse's aide

5. I/machine shop
   1985–1989
   mechanic

6. she/electronics company
   1987–1993
   assembler

7. she/furniture company
   1979–1989
   carpenter

8. he/high school
   1981–1991
   teacher

9. he/construction company
   1984–1990
   engineer

Complete these statements about work experience.

1. They ___*worked*___ in a machine shop ___*from*___ 1988 ___*to*___ 1991.
   They ___*were*___ machinists.

2. He _____ in a construction company _____ 1987
   _____ 1988.
   He _____ an engineer.

3. She _____ in a warehouse _____ 1985 _____ 1990.
   She _____ a quality control inspector.

4. They _____ in a hospital _____ 1986 _____ 1992.
   They _____ practical nurses.

CONCEN TRATION **Cut out and play the Concentration Game on page 95. Match each picture with the correct sentence.**

Talk about the previous experience of each person.

Student 1

machine shop   mechanic
I worked in a machine shop.
I was a mechanic.

1. machine shop
   mechanic
2. he/drug company
   shipping clerk
3. they/bank
   tellers
4. I/hospital
   nurse
5. she/toy factory
   assembler
6. they/airport
   food service handlers

(FOLD HERE)

Student 2
**Listen carefully and help Student 1
say the sentence correctly.**

1. I worked in a machine shop.
   I was a mechanic.
2. He worked in a drug company.
   He was a shipping clerk.
3. They worked in a bank.
   They were tellers.
4. I worked in a hospital.
   I was a nurse.
5. She worked in a toy factory.
   She was an assembler.
6. They worked in an airport.
   They were food service handlers.

Complete these sentences about your work experience.

1. Tell me about your job.

   I work in a _____.

   I am a/an _____.

2. Tell me about your previous experience.

   I worked in a _____ from _____ to _____.

   I was a/an _____.

   I worked in a _____ from _____ to _____.

   I was a/an _____.

Ask three students these questions about their jobs. Fill in their answers on the chart below.

QUESTIONS	STUDENT 1	STUDENT 2	STUDENT 3
Where do you work?			
What do you do?			
Where did you work before this?			
What did you do?			

Putting It Together

Alex is applying for a job as shipping manager in a large import company. This is part of the job application form. Discuss the questions below.

NAME AND ADDRESS OF EMPLOYER	FROM	TO	POSITION	REASON FOR LEAVING
Berkeley Drugs *Los Angeles, Calif.*	*9/90*	*Present*	*shipping clerk*	*seeking supervisory position*
Clark Manufacturing *Los Angeles, Calif.*	*7/88*	*9/90*	*machine operator*	*better job*
La Casita *Mexico City, Mexico*	*11/86*	*6/88*	*sales clerk*	*moved to USA*

Discuss these questions about the job application form.

1. Where does Alex work?
2. What does he do?
3. When did he start his job?
4. How long has he been working at his present job?
5. Where did he work from 7/88 to 9/90?
6. What did he do?
7. How long did he work there?
8. Why did he leave?
9. What did he do in his country?
10. What company did he work for?
11. How long did he work there?
12. Why did he leave?

Complete this job application about your own work experience.

NAME AND ADDRESS OF EMPLOYER	FROM	TO	POSITION	REASON FOR LEAVING

Role play

With another student, write a short job interview between an employer and a job applicant. Ask about the applicant's previous experience. Ask for company names, dates of employment, and positions. Present your dialogue to the class.

15 Job Responsibilities

Did you ever go on a job interview?
What questions did the interviewer ask you?
What kinds of jobs can you find in this area?
What kind of job would you like in the future?

Listen, Read and Say

Interviewer: Are you working?
Maria: No, I'm going to school full time. But I was a payroll clerk for three years before that.
Interviewer: What were your responsibilities?
Maria: I kept the records and did the payroll.

Practice this conversation with the following jobs.

> *He was a bookkeeper.* _____ .
> *He did the payroll.* _____ .

1. he/bookkeeper
   do the payroll

2. I/sewing machine operator
   make dresses

3. he/high school teacher
   teach Spanish

4. she/saleswoman
   sell clothing

5. I/truck driver
   drive a tractor trailer

6. she/medical technician
   take x-rays

58

Practice **Practice**

Practice this conversation with the following jobs.

A: What did _____ she _____ do in _____ her _____ country?
B: _____ She _____ was _____ a secretary. _____.
_____ She typed letters and reports. _____.

1. she/secretary
   type letters and reports

2. he/mechanic
   fix cars

3. she/beautician
   style hair

4. I/nurse
   work in pediatrics

5. he/shipping clerk
   pack and ship orders

6. they/assembly line
   workers
   assemble radios

Partner Exercise

Talk about each person's previous experience.

Student 1	**Student 2**
I/bookkeeper keep the records	**Listen carefully and help Student 1 say the sentence correctly.**
I was a bookkeeper. I kept the records.	

1. I/bookkeeper
   keep the records
2. I/insurance agent
   sell insurance policies
3. They/nurses
   specialize in emergency care

4. He/mechanic
   repair cars
5. She/shipping clerk
   pack and ship orders
6. I/quality control inspector
   check machine parts
7. She/accountant
   fill out tax returns
8. He/supervisor
   supervise production

(FOLD HERE)

1. I was a bookkeeper.
   I kept the records.
2. I was an insurance agent.
   I sold insurance policies.
3. They were nurses.
   They specialized in emergency care.
4. He was a mechanic.
   He repaired cars.
5. She was a shipping clerk.
   She packed and shipped orders.
6. I was a quality control inspector.
   I checked machine parts.
7. She was an accountant.
   She filled out tax returns.
8. He was a supervisor.
   He supervised production.

Complete these sentences about the work experience of these people.

1. I __was__ a mechanic.   I _repaired_ diesel engines.
2. She _____ a receptionist.   She _____ the telephone.
3. He _____ a barber.   He _____ hair.
4. She _____ a high school teacher. She _____ math.
5. They _____ medical technicians. They _____ x-rays.
6. He _____ a nurse.   He _____ in cardiac care.
7. I _____ a taxi driver.   I _____ a cab in Madrid.
8. They _____ secretaries.   They _____ letters.
9. He _____ an assembly line worker. He _____ computers.
10. She _____ a real estate agent. She _____ houses.

Complete these sentences about your work experience and responsibilities.

1. I am a _____.
2. I _____ and _____.
3. I was a _____.
4. I _____ and _____.
5. In my country, I was a _____.
6. I _____ and _____.

Ask two students these questions about their work experience. Fill in their answers on the chart below.

Interaction

QUESTIONS	STUDENT 1	STUDENT 2
Where do you work?		
What do you do?		
What are your responsibilities?		
Where did you work before this?		
What did you do?		
What were your duties?		

Teresa is applying for a job as a teller in a bank. Who is she talking to? What is she wearing? What questions is the interviewer asking her? What questions is Teresa going to ask her?

Discuss these interview questions. Talk about your own job experience.

1. Where are you working now?
2. What's your position?
3. What are your responsibilities?
4. Where did you work before this?
5. Did you work in your country? What did you do?
6. What special skills do you have?
7. Why do you want this job?
8. Why do you want to leave your present job?

Role play

With another student, write a short job interview between an employer and a job applicant. Ask about the applicant's present and previous job experience and responsibilities. Present your dialogue to the class.

16 Community Resources

Discuss

Do you have a library card?
When was the last time you went to the Motor Vehicle Agency?
What other community services and agencies does your town have? Did you ever use any of their services?

Listen, Read and Say

Daniel: I called you yesterday morning, but you were out.
Amy: I went to the Motor Vehicle Agency. I had to wait in line two hours just to register my car.
Daniel: I told you not to wait until the last day of the month.

Practice Practice

Practice both models with each picture.

| _____**He**_____ was at _the post office_ . | _____**He**_____ went to _the post office_ . |

1. he/yesterday

2. I/this morning

3. they/yesterday afternoon

4. he/last night

5. she/two days ago

6. we/this afternoon

62

Practice this model and ask about each person's activities at these community agencies.

> A: What did ___David___ do yesterday?
>
> B: ___He___ went to the ___library___ and ___returned some books.___

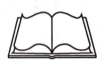

LIBRARY		
David return some books pay a small fine	**Martha** get a library card take out some books	**Leroy** get information about buying a tv

MOTOR VEHICLE AGENCY		
Martin renew license renew registration	**Magda** take written test get learner's permit	**Kim** apply for a license

CLINIC		
Marc apply for the Family Health Clinic	**Carlos** get the results of his blood tests	**Sherri** have her six-month prenatal check-up

CITY HALL—RECREATION DEPARTMENT		
Howard join the city pool	**Terry** register her son for summer day camp	**Shirley** get a tennis permit

POLICE DEPARTMENT		
Anna report a mugging	**Al** file a complaint	**Orlando** fill out an accident report

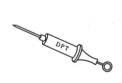

BOARD OF HEALTH		
Maria get a marriage license	**Gloria** get immunizations for her children	**Charles** complain about mice in his apartment building

What did each person do yesterday?

Student 1	**Student 2**
She/renew her license	*Listen carefully and help Student 1*
She renewed her license.	*say the sentence correctly.*

Student 1	Student 2
1. She/renew her license	1. She renewed her license.
2. He/send a package	2. He sent a package.
3. They/get a marriage license	3. They got a marriage license.
4. She/fill out an accident report	4. She filled out an accident report.
5. We/got tennis permits	5. We got tennis permits.
6. He/have an EKG	6. He had an EKG.
7. I/register my child for school	7. I registered my child for school.
8. She/apply for a license	8. She applied for a license.

(FOLD HERE)

Complete the first blank with** was, were, or went. **In the second blank, write the correct verb in the past tense.

1. I _____was_____ at the post office and ____bought____ some stamps.
2. They _____ at the recreation department and _____ the city pool.
3. He _____ to the police station and _____ a mugging.
4. She _____ at the library and _____ out some books.
5. We _____ to the Board of Health and _____ immunizations for our children.
6. I _____ to the Motor Vehicle Agency and _____ the road test.
7. She _____ to the clinic and _____ a check-up with the obstetrician.

Ask another student these questions about community agencies. Fill in the information on the chart below.

Did you ever go to _____?
What did you do there?

PLACE	YES/NO	ACTIVITY
the Post Office	Yes No	
the Motor Vehicle Agency	Yes No	
the Library	Yes No	
City Hall	Yes No	
the Board of Health	Yes No	
the Police Department	Yes No	

These are six departments in a local City Hall. What does each department offer to the residents of a town? Where is each person? What is each person asking? Write the new vocabulary on the picture.

Role play

Work in a small group. For the next class, find out the following information about your city or town. Share your information with the class.

AGENCY	LOCATION	HOURS	TELEPHONE
Police Department			
Fire Department			
Rescue Squad			
City Hall			
Motor Vehicle			
Board of Health			

17 Personal Information

Discuss

Where were you born? Where did you grow up?
When did you come to the United States?
Where did you live when you first came to the United States?

Listen, Read and Say

Hector: Hi. My name is Hector. You're in my English class.
Nelson: Yes, I'm Nelson Cruz. Where are you from?
Hector: Cali, Colombia.
Nelson: When did you come to the United States?
Hector: I came in 1989.
Nelson: When did you start to study English?
Hector: I started last year.
Nelson: I began this year. Well, it's nice to meet you.
Hector: Nice to meet you, too.

Practice
Practice

Ask and answer questions about Nelson's life story.

A: _____*Where did he grow up*_____?
B: _____*He grew up in Mexico City*_____.

MEXICO CITY

1. Where/grow up

1985

2. When/graduate from high school

BANK

3. Where/find his first job

66

1987

NEW JERSEY

4. When/move to the U.S. 5. Where/get a job 6. Where/rent an apartment

1987

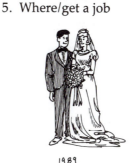
1989

1990

7. Where/meet his wife 8. When/get married 9. When/have their first child

1990

1991

10. Where/begin to study English 11. When/become a supervisor 12. When/finish his English classes

Partner Exercise

Ask and answer these questions about Kyoko.

Student 1

Where/Kyoko/grow up?
Where did Kyoko grow up?

Student 2
Listen carefully and help Student 1 say the sentence correctly.

(FOLD HERE)

Student 1	Student 2
1. Where/Kyoko grow up?	1. Where did Kyoko grow up?
2. She/grow up in Japan.	2. She grew up in Japan.
3. When/graduate from high school?	3. When did she graduate from high school?
4. She/graduate in 1988.	4. She graduated in 1988.
5. Where/get her first job?	5. Where did she get her first job?
6. She/get it in an office.	6. She got it in an office.
7. When/move to the U.S.?	7. When did she move to the U.S.?
8. She/move in 1992.	8. She moved in 1992.
9. When/begin English classes?	9. When did she begin English classes?
10. She/begin them in 1993.	10. She began them in 1993.

Complete this paragraph about Ana.

Ana was born in Poland and she _____**grew**_____ (grow) up in Gdansk, near the Baltic Sea. She _____ (graduate) from high school in 1984. One year later, she _____ (move) to the United States with her parents. They _____ (find) an apartment in Chicago, Illinois. A few months later, Ana _____ (begin) English classes at a community college in her neighborhood. In 1986, she _____ (get) her first job in an office. The same year, Ana _____ (meet) her husband at work. They _____ (be) married in 1988. They _____ (have) their first child in 1990. Ana _____ (receive) a degree in Accounting Data Processing in 1992.

Complete these sentences about your own life.

1. I _____ (be) born in 19_____.
2. I _____ (grow) up in _____.
3. I _____ (come) to the United States in _____.
4. I _____ (begin) to study English in _____.
5. I _____ (get) married in _____.

Interaction

Ask two students these questions about their lives. Fill in their answers on the chart below.

QUESTION	STUDENT 1	STUDENT 2
Where were you born?		
Where did you grow up?		
When did you come to the U.S.?		
Where did you live when you came to the U.S.?		
When did you begin to study English?		

This time line tells about important events in Leon's life. Talk about each date in Leon's life.

1960	be born in Haitien, Haiti
1963	move to Port-au-Prince
1978	graduate from high school
1980	come to Houston, Texas
1981	begin to study English
1982	meet his wife
1983	begin to study Computer Science
1984	get married
1985	move to Orlando, Florida
1986	start work in an electronics company
1987	have a daughter
1989	finish his degree in Computer Science
1990	buy a house
1992	change jobs begin to work for a large corporation

Discuss these questions about the information in the time line.

1. When was Leon born? Where did he grow up?
2. What did he study before he studied computer science?
3. How long did he live in Houston, Texas?
4. When did he meet his wife?
5. How long did he know his wife before they got married?
6. When did they have their first child? How old is she now?
7. How long did he work at the electronics company?
8. Where did they buy a house?
9. Where is he working now?
10. How long has he been in the United States?

Role play

Write a time line for your life. Write one sentence for each important date. Then, work with another student or a small group and talk about your time line. Ask and answer questions about the information.

18 Going to the Doctor

Discuss

Do you have a family doctor?
When was the last time you went
   to a doctor?
What was the matter with you?
How did you feel?
Did the doctor prescribe any
   medication?

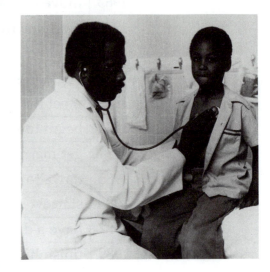

Listen, Read and Say

Gloria: My son is sick.
Doctor: What's the matter with him?
Gloria: He has a cold and is very congested.
Doctor: Does he have a fever?
Gloria: Yes, he does. It's 102°.

Practice
Practice

Practice this model with the symptoms below.

He's sick .	*They're tired* .

1. he/sick   2. they/tired   3. she/achy all over   4. I/nauseous

5. I/dizzy   6. I/congested   7. he/constipated   8. she/very pale

Practice this model with the symptoms below.

| _____ **I** _____ have _____ **a sore throat** _____. | _____ **She** _____ has _____ **a fever** _____. |

1. I/a sore throat   2. she/a fever   3. he/a stomachache

4. she/a cough   6. I/a cold   7. he/the flu

8. she/a runny nose   9. she/diarrhea   10. I/a rash

Partner Exercise

Describe each health problem.

Student 1

I/a fever
I have a fever.

1. I/a fever
2. She/a stomachache
3. He/nauseous
4. They/the flu
5. She/constipated
6. We/tired
7. He/dizzy
8. She/temperature
9. I/achy all over
10. He/congested

(FOLD HERE)

Student 2
Listen carefully and help Student 1 say the sentence correctly.

1. I have a fever.
2. She has a stomachache.
3. He's nauseous.
4. They have the flu.
5. She's constipated.
6. We're tired.
7. He's dizzy.
8. She has a temperature.
9. I'm achy all over.
10. He's congested.

CONCEN TRATION   **Play the Concentration Game on page 97. Match the health problem with the correct sentence.**

Fill in the temperature on each thermometer.

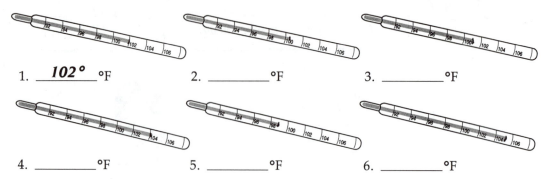

1. **102°** °F

2. _____ °F

3. _____ °F

4. _____ °F

5. _____ °F

6. _____ °F

Complete these conversations between a parent and a nurse. Write a problem and a temperature.

1. Henry: My daughter is sick.
   Nurse: What's the problem?
   Henry: She's _____**dizzy**_____.
   Nurse: Does she have a fever?
   Henry: Yes, she **does**. It's **101°**

2. Kyoko: My son is sick.
   Nurse: What's the problem?
   Kyoko: He has _____.
   Nurse: Does he have a fever?
   Kyoko: Yes, he ____. It's ____.

3. Marie: My son is sick.
   Nurse: What's the problem?
   Marie: He's _____.
   Nurse: Does he have a fever?
   Marie: Yes, he ____. It's ____.

4. Eric: My daughter is sick.
   Nurse: What's the matter?
   Eric: She has _____.
   Nurse: Does she have a fever?
   Eric: No, she _____.

Interaction

Ask another student these questions about going to the doctor. Fill in the information on the chart below.

When was the last time you went to _____?
Where did you go?
How much is an office visit?

DOCTOR	DATE	PLACE	COST
a family doctor			
a dentist			
an optometrist			
a pediatrician			

72

John is sick. He is weak and congested. He has a fever and a bad cough. He went to the doctor this morning. Talk about the examination. What did the doctor do? Write the new vocabulary on the picture.

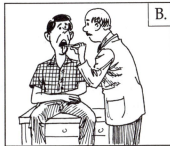
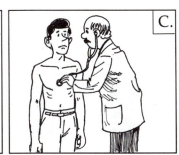
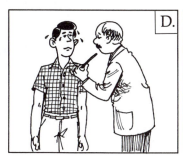

Match these expressions with the correct picture above.

_____ 1. Roll up your sleeve and give me your arm.

_____ 2. Take this three times a day with lots of water.

_____ 3. Hold your breath and don't move.

_____ 4. Say AHHHHH!

_____ 5. Keep this under your tongue.

_____ 6. Breathe in. Breathe out.

Role play

With another student, write a short conversation between a doctor and a patient in the examination room. Find out the symptoms and give a diagnosis. Give the patient some medical advice and write a prescription, if necessary. Present your dialogue to the class.

19 Your Children's Health

Discuss

When your child is sick, do you need to call the school?

Can you pick up your children's homework when they are sick?

When your child goes back to school, do you write an absence note?

Did your children miss any days of school this year? Why?

Listen, Read and Say

10/13

Dear Mrs. Johnson,

Michael was absent from school on 10/12. He cut his arm and needed six stitches. Please excuse him from gym activities for one week. Enclosed is the doctor's note.

Thank you.

Sincerely,

William Vega

Practice **Practice**

Practice this model with the problems below.

My _____ **daughter** _____ had _____ **a bad cough** _____.

1. daughter
   a bad cough

2. son
   an ear infection

3. children
   the chicken pox

4. son
   an upset stomach

5. daughter
   a bad rash

6. son
   the measles

Practice this model with the problems below.

My ___daughter___ ___broke her arm___.

1. daughter
   break her arm

2. son
   pull a muscle

3. son
   burn his hand

4. daughter
   sprain her ankle

5. daughter
   fall and hit her head

6. son
   hurt his back

7. son
   have a doctor's
   appointment

8. daughter
   step on a piece of glass
   and need six stitches

9. son
   cut his finger and need
   four stitches

Complete these sentences with the verb in the past time.

1. My daughter ___had___ (have) an upset stomach.

2. My son _____ (step) on a broken bottle and _____ (cut) his foot. He _____ (need) four stitches.

3. My daughter _____ (fall) and _____ (hit) her head.

4. My son _____ (have) a dentist's appointment.

5. My son _____ (have) a bad cough and a cold.

6. My daughter _____ (pull) a muscle in her leg.

7. My daughter _____ (cut) her arm and _____ (need) twenty stitches.

8. My son _____ (break) his arm.

9. My daughter _____ (have) the flu and a high fever.

10. My daughter _____ (sprain) her wrist.

Cut out and play the Concentration Game on page 99. Match each problem with the correct sentence.

Partner Exercise

Describe the health problem.

Student 1	**Student 2**
son/break his leg	*Listen carefully and help Student 1*
My son broke his leg.	*say the sentence correctly.*

Student 1	Student 2
1. son/break his leg	1. My son broke his leg.
2. daughter/sprain her ankle	2. My daughter sprained her ankle.
3. daughter/have a rash	3. My daughter had a rash.
4. daughter/hurt her back	4. My daughter hurt her back.
5. son/cut his toe	5. My son cut his toe.
6. son/have/the chicken pox	6. My son had the chicken pox.
7. son/fall and hit his head	7. My son fell and hit his head.
8. daughter/burn her hand	8. My daughter burned her hand.
9. daughter/pull a muscle	9. My daughter pulled a muscle.
10. son/have/an ear infection	10. My son had an ear infection.

(FOLD HERE)

Interaction

Ask three students these questions about their family's health. Fill in their answers on the chart below.

Was anyone in your family absent from school or work recently?
What was the problem?

PERSON	PROBLEM

Read these two notes that Mrs. Lee wrote the school about her children's absences. Discuss the questions below each note.

11/15

Dear Ms. Lawson,
   Melissa was absent from 11/2 to 11/14. She had the chicken pox. Thank you.
                              Sincerely,
                              Kim Lee

4/4

Dear Mr. Bond,
   Sang was absent on 4/2 and 4/3. He fell off his bicycle and broke his arm. Please excuse him from gym activities for one month. Enclosed is the doctor's note. Thank you.
                              Sincerely,
                              Kim Lee

1. What's the date on the note?
2. What's the teacher's name?
3. When was Melissa absent?
4. What was the matter?

1. What's the date on the note?
2. Who's the teacher?
3. When did Sang miss school?
4. What was the problem?
5. What can't Sang do?

Your children were sick and missed school. Write notes in these boxes.

With another student, write a telephone conversation between a parent and the secretary at school. Explain why your child is absent. Present your dialogue to the class.

20 Telephone

Discuss

Do you ever take or leave messages
on the telephone?
When you call and get an answering
machine, do you leave a message?
How often do you make long distance
phone calls?
When are the best times to call
long distance?

Listen, Read and Say

Wilma:	Hello.
Thomas:	Hello. This is Thomas Gomez. Can I speak to Mr. Jefferson?
Wilma:	He's not here right now. He's out to lunch.
Thomas:	Please ask him to call me. My phone number is 482-6930.

Practice
Practice

Practice this model with the pictures below. Use your name in the model.

> A: This is _____.
>   I'd like to speak to __*Mr. Bean*__.
> B: I'm sorry. __*He*__ is __*out of the office*__.

1. Mr. Bean
   out of the office

2. Mrs. Temple
   out to lunch

3. Mrs. Stoll
   out sick

4. Mrs. Griffin
   on vacation

5. Mr. Morales
   on another line

6. Mr. Marraffi
   at a meeting

78

Receptionist: Good morning. Urban Insurance.
Michael: This is Michael Polski. I'd like to speak to Mr. Blake.
Receptionist: I'm sorry. He's out of the office.
Michael: Please ask him to call me.

Practice this model with your name. Ask to speak to these people.

A: This is _____.
Can I speak to _**Mr. Hanson**_ ?
B: _**He**_ 's not here right now.
A: Please ask _**him**_ to call me.

A: This is _____.
Can I speak to _**Mrs. Costa**_ ?
B: _**She**_ 's not here right now.
A: Please ask _**her**_ to call me.

1. Mr. Hanson

2. Mrs. Costra

3. Ms. Davis

4. Robert Short

5. Wilson Chavez

6. Kim Lee

Complete these telephone conversations.

A: This __*is*__ Sam Fuller. __*Can*__ I speak to Laura?
B: __*She's*__ out of the office right now.
A: Please ask _____ _**her to call me**_ _____.

A: This _____ Edward Yossim. _____ I speak to Bill?
B: _____ out sick today.
A: Please ask _____.

A: This _____ Paulina Rose. _____ I speak to Mr. Charles?
B: _____ at a meeting.
A: Please ask _____.

A: This _____ Larry Mitsall. _____ I speak to Barbara?
B: _____ on vacation this week.
A: Please ask _____.

Practice this model with the information in the chart below. Use your name and telephone number.

A: Good _____*morning*_____. Alcan Corporation.
B: I'd like to speak to _____*Mr. Ball*_____.
A: I'm sorry. _____*He's on vacation*_____. Can I take a message?
B: Yes. This is _____. Please ask __*him*__ to call me at _____.

A	B	A	B
morning	Mr. Ball	on vacation	Yes.
afternoon	Mrs. Triano	out of the office	Yes.
evening	Ms. Jackson	out sick	No, I'll call back later.
morning	Rita Stevens	at a meeting	Yes.
evening	Eric Pepper	out to lunch	No, I'll call back later.
afternoon	Kevin Lawson	on another line	Yes.

Complete these conversations.

Secretary: Good ___*afternoon*___. Kline Photography.
 Caller: _____*I'd like to*_____ speak to Mr. Kline.
Secretary: I'm sorry. He __*'s at a meeting*_____.
 Can I _____*take a message*_____?
 Caller: Yes, this is _____. Please tell __*him*__ that the meeting at
 2:00 is cancelled.

Secretary: Good _____. Speedy Printing.
 Caller: _____ speak to Lisa Miller.
Secretary: I'm sorry. She _____.
 _____ a message?
 Caller: Yes, this is _____ from Lincoln School. Please tell
 _____ that her daughter is sick.

Secretary: Good _____. Best Painting.
 Caller: _____ speak to David Welsh.
Secretary: I'm sorry. _____.
 _____ a message?
 Caller: Yes, this is _____. I would like an estimate on a painting
 job at my house.

This is the long-distance section of Sharon Johnson's telephone bill. What information does each column give?

June 15			DETAIL OF ITEMIZED CALLS		908-965-3029	583	42	
NO.	DATE	TIME	PLACE		AREA—NUMBER	RATE	MIN	AMOUNT
1.	MAY 13	10:58PM	TO DURHAM	NC	919 490-1146	E	1 T	.14
2.	MAY 14	8:49AM	TO MERCERYL	NJ	609 588-2424	D	1 T	.20
3.	MAY 14	3:23PM	TO DURHAM	NC	909 490-1146	D	2 T	.44
4.	MAY 15	7:12PM	TO CHESTERTN	NY	518 494-2956	E	29 T	4.89
5.	MAY 21	11:21AM	TO ANNAPOLIS	MD	301 243-8591	D	10 T	2.78
6.	MAY 26	11:56PM	TO DURHAM	NC	919 490-1146	N	2 T	.24
7.	MAY 29	7:08AM	TO QUEENS	NY	718 227-5646	N	8 T	.88
8.	JUN 2	8:40PM	TO CHESTER	PA	215 872-4267	D	1 T	.21
9.	JUN 6	10:16AM	TO NEW YORK	NY	212 571-0267	E	1 T	.11
10.	JUN 6	3:18PM	TO MIAMI	FL	305 865-2000	E	17 T	3.23
11.	JUN 8	5:02PM	TO PALALTO	CA	415 634-3426	E	4 T	.60
12.	JUN 8	8:43PM	TO BRNWICH	CT	203 627-6020	E	5 T	.65
13.	JUN 10	3:12PM	TO DURHAM	NC	919 490-1146	D	3 T	.66
						Total		15.03

1. How much was the phone call to Durham, North Carolina, on May 13?
2. What time did Sharon make the call?
3. How long was the phone call?
4. What city does Sharon often call?
5. How many night calls did she make this month?
6. What was the longest call Sharon made? How much did it cost?
7. What states did Sharon call?
8. How much was Sharon's long distance bill for the month?
9. What's the night rate per minute to Durham, North Carolina? What's the day rate? What's the evening rate?
10. Why do you think she got the evening rate for some calls during the day?
11. What long distance service do you have?
12. For your long distance phone company, what are the hours for the day rate, the evening rate, the night rate?

Role play

With another student, write a telephone conversation between a receptionist and a caller. The person you are calling is not in. Leave a message for that person. Present your dialogue to the class.

IRREGULAR PAST VERBS

be	was, were	hold	held
become	became	hurt	hurt
begin	began	keep	kept
break	broke	leave	left
bring	brought	lend	lent
build	built	lie	lay
buy	bought	make	made
catch	caught	meet	met
come	came	pay	paid
cost	cost	read	read
cut	cut	ring	rang
do	did	say	said
drink	drank	see	saw
eat	ate	sell	sold
fall	fell	send	sent
feel	felt	sing	sang
find	found	sleep	slept
fight	fought	speak	spoke
fly	flew	spend	spent
get	got	stand	stood
give	gave	take	took
go	went	teach	taught
grew	grow	tell	told
have	had	think	thought
hear	heard	write	wrote
hit	hit		

Concentration Games

UNIT 2 ■ AROUND THE HOUSE

		He's mopping the floor.
		She's making the bed.
		They're doing the laundry.
		She's paying the bills.
		He's watching tv.
		She's reading.
		They're playing cards.
		They're studying.

UNIT 3 ■ HOUSING PROBLEMS

		The air-conditioner isn't working.
		The stove isn't working.
		The light switch isn't working.
		The dishwasher isn't working.
		The faucet is leaking.
		The toilet is overflowing.
		The ceiling is leaking.
		The plaster is falling.

UNIT 4 ■ THE WEEKEND

I	I	I'm going to go to the park.
		I'm going to look for a new tv.
We	He	We're going to have a party.
		He's going to fix his car.
They	He	They're going to eat out.
		He's going to play soccer.
She	She	She's going to watch tv.
		She's going to go shopping.

		He plays with cars and trucks.
		He learns letters and numbers.
		He takes a nap.
		He paints.
		They sing songs.
		They play games.
		They build with blocks.
		They take walks.

lend	borrow	Can you lend me a quarter?
		Can I borrow a dollar?
lend	lend	Can you lend me a dollar?
		Can you lend me five dollars?
borrow	borrow	Can I borrow five dollars?
		Can I borrow ten dollars?
lend	borrow	Can you lend me ten dollars?
		Can I borrow twenty dollars?

UNIT 11 ■ THE DELI

1/2 lb.	1/4 lb.	a half a pound *or* a half pound
		a quarter of a pound *or* a quarter pound
3/4 lb.	1 lb.	three quarters of a pound
		one pound
1 1/2 lbs.	3 1/2 lbs.	a pound and a half
		three and a half pounds
1 1/4 lbs.	2 1/2 lbs.	a pound and a quarter
		two and a half pounds

UNIT 13 ■ SHOPPING

		The collar is stained.
		A button is missing.
		The seam is torn (ripped).
		The zipper is broken.
		The pocket is ripped (torn).
		The leg is stained.
		The sleeve is stained.
		The cuff is stained.

UNIT 14 ■ WORK EXPERIENCE

They	She	They were security guards.
		She was an x-ray technician.
I	He	I was a hi-lo operator.
		He was an electrician.
I	She	I was a machine operator.
		She was a nurse's aide.
They	He	They were data entry clerks.
		He was a mechanic.

UNIT 18 ■ GOING TO THE DOCTOR

I	I	I'm nauseous.
		I'm dizzy.
He	She	He's congested.
		She has a sore throat.
She	He	She has a cough.
		He has a stomachache.
She	He	She has a fever.
		He has a rash.

UNIT 19 ■ YOUR CHILDREN'S HEALTH

		She broke her arm.
		He pulled a muscle.
		He burned his hand.
		She sprained her ankle.
		She fell and hit her head.
		He hurt his back.
		She stepped on a piece of glass.
		He cut his finger.